Daylight

Sunlight on the Garden: Travelling with the poetry
of Louis MacNeice

Daylight

Nine months of not writing a bestseller

Z. W. BATES

Published in paperback in Great Britain in 2014 by Carr Design Studio.

Copyright © Zillah Stone, 2014.

The moral right of Zillah Stone to be identified as the author of this work has been asserted by her under the Copyright, Designs and Patents Act of 1988.

A CIP catalogue record for this book is available from the British Library.

ISBN: 978-0-9929201-1-1

Printed and bound in Great Britain using FSC Mix materials.
Designed and typeset in Bembo by Carr Design Studio.

Cover photographs by Zillah Stone.
Front: from Isafjordur to its harbour and airport.
Back: author's shadow on containership, New York leaves.

Contents

'It is foolish to ask for ease but we ask for adequacy that we may cope. We ask not for a smooth sea but for a well set compass and strong courage'

written by my maternal grandfather
just before he died on 3 September 1962

~

To my sister – who knew (before I did)
that I would write a book one day

With thanks to all my family and friends who support
me, and with particular thanks to those whose confidence
re-inflated me when I was compressed

1

Prologue

So here's the plan. I hand in my notice and leave the job I have been enjoying for the last six years. I give myself one year to see if I can actually write a book – as opposed to thinking about one day writing a book. And then I go back to what I have been doing for the last 20-something years, working as a company secretary and corporate lawyer.

I know that conventional wisdom says you should not give up the day job to write, but then I do not have the evenings and weekends in my day job that conventional wisdom assumes.

Yes it does sound a bit improbable, but before I even wrote those first two paragraphs I took the first step. I handed in my notice. Any journey starts with the cliché of the first step.

And improbable is not to be confused with impossible. I recognise conventional wisdom has a point and I know there is never an ideal time to defy conventional wisdom, but this seems as good a time as any.

So back to my plan: I have set myself nine months to research, travel and write and then three months to edit and do, or have done, all that which turns text into a book for publication. Provisional title *Sunlight on the Garden: Travelling with the poetry of*

Louis MacNeice. In my head it will be a travel book hooked on various places that are associated with Louis MacNeice, the poet born in Belfast, a Classics lecturer who became a radio producer for the BBC and died in 1963.

The first part of my book's title comes from one of MacNeice's more famous poems, called *The Sunlight on the Garden.* I say more famous advisedly, for although his work has perhaps had a resurgence of interest since I 'found' him when I was a teenager in the 1980s, he is unlikely to be a household name, even in a household that names poets.

I am a lawyer both by training and inclination, given to categorising and planning, but *Sunlight* will not be a comprehensive biography. It will be a partial book, in both the sense of being only a part and in the sense of being biased. It will be a personal account of my travels in 2013 to places associated with Louis MacNeice; it will give me the opportunity to see more daylight than I have for the past 20-something years.

As I type up this first draft I am looking out over my garden in south London, where it is raining and the clouds are unvarying in their greyness, but still it makes a change from looking inwards, into an office.

And yes, I know *Sunlight* will not be a bestseller, but unless I write it no one will be able to read it, no one will be able to share my enjoyment of Louis MacNeice's poetry while travelling through everyday places and past mildly improbable places, and I will never know if I could have written a book.

In the corporate world there is some reality within the idea that what is reported on gets done, so coming into this new world

I have decided I will make a diary note with myself to sit down once every five days and report to myself on what I have done or am planning. I will write about that day, or about the four days before or the next four days, or perhaps just about the view from my desk at the moment I stop being in the continuous present to write about that one instant. Gradually over my nine months of writing, layer by layer, I will build up a record of what those nine months were like, at the time, before they were overlaid with the patina of hindsight.

That way, even if *Sunlight* gets no further than being an idea in my head, I will still be able to write one book, which I can get printed and at the end of my writing year take down from my own bookshelves.

So there you have it.

That's the plan.

I am stepping out of the corporate world I have known to try something else, to have a writing year. I have spreadsheets and lists to help order my thoughts and budget my money, and indeed budget that scarce resource of time, but it comes down to me and a keyboard and building up words to make paragraphs and then chapters and ultimately a book (or two) that I will leave behind.

When they heard what I was planning to do some people said I was brave, with a slight hint of wistfulness in their voice, wishing they could do the same. Some people were completely without reaction – it was such an odd thing to do, it was beyond comprehension or comment. Some people reacted with 'wow' or even, if they were of that age, 'cool'. For them it sounded like a pretty improbable thing to be doing, but when they thought about the people they knew who might do something improbable, I was quite high up their list.

What of Louis MacNeice? When I told people what I was planning to do, there were very few of my friends or work colleagues who had heard of him. One who had heard of him, knew him from seeing a blue plaque on the front of a house in Canonbury, north London, marking where he had lived from 1947 to 1952. She volunteered me to write a 500-word article for a local magazine, run by volunteers, so no money, just the first chance to see my name in print.

Ah – yes. I paused at that idea.

My name. My writing name. What name was I going to put into print? On the one hand there is the company secretary and corporate lawyer who works in London and on the proverbial other hand there is the writer, closely related. Both use words as their stock in trade and choose them with care, but the writer might indulge in metaphorical flights of fancy, twirl in a sweepingly unqualified generalisation or three to illustrate a point far more colourfully than the lawyer would ever dare to. Would the writer be freer to be her own person if she had a different name from that of the lawyer? Like sending two daughters who are different to two different schools, so neither is in the shadow of the other?

Since the writer and the lawyer are so closely related I decided to keep some things the same. Z whether you spell it aloud as 'zed' or 'zee' stands out, but it is my first initial. It may look exotic, but the reality is I am not exotic. Medium height, medium build, brown eyes, mid-brown hair with increasing flecks of grey. I have no obvious fieldmarks, but I am Z, Z for mildly improbable.

So what about a new surname? A writing surname. On both sides of the family I come from practical stock: doing and making, though not necessarily doing and making what and how others did and made. On my father's side there was the story of a grandfather who was a farmer and corn merchant, who bought a lorry, when such things were unusual in his part of the west of England. On my mother's side there was a recurrency of printers and crafters of words. That grandfather was the general manager of a factory printing cardboard boxes, whose sermons as a non-conformist lay preacher were remembered, by those who had heard them, decades after his early death.

I am my own person, but in recognition of my inheritance I decided to re-use the surname of a past generation: Bates.

With my writing name decided, I sat down at my keyboard one Saturday morning, before I had planned to, before I had left my job and while, unusually for the winter of 2013, the sun shone through my window, I typed.

There was, though, a shadow, the shadow of the possibility of an untidiness intervening and smudging the neatness of my plan. After a routine medical test, I had been recalled for a closer examination of an indeterminate area.

While I waited for the next appointment, for the determination of the indeterminate area, putting words down and concentrating on their order seemed the most useful thing to do. Well maybe not useful, in the way a corn merchant replacing a horse and cart with a lorry was useful, but more useful than worrying about what a closer examination might reveal.

I applied myself to the requested 500 words. 600 words later I stood up. I refreshed my coffee and returned to prune and edit.

Looking at my morning's typing mathematically I concluded an hour and a half for 500 words made three hours for 1,000 words on a good day. A simple sum said 240 hours for my self-appointed hurdle of a book being 80,000 words. 240 hours to write a first draft and refine a second draft.

Five hours a day in a five-day week would give me time to do more than type. It would give wriggle room to have some fun amid the punctuation; some breakfast and supper with those still inside the corporate world; perhaps some lunch and coffee outside in the daylight (when it was not raining).

From the point of view of a spreadsheet that added up to a practicable proposition. Two and a half months of typing at a steady rate before adding the thinking, the structuring, the making of connections and the stripping back of complexity; the preparing to travel, the experiencing of travel, the digesting of travel; and the reading around the work of others as well as the reading over of my own.

The lawyer in me reviewed the evidence submitted by the writer and agreed the writer's plan was grounded in what appeared to be a workable reality.

The company secretary (with more than a decade of writing and producing annual reports) submitted that, as a rule of thumb, seven, not two, drafts are required. The first three drafts each need a lot of amendments, the next two are more tidying up for internal consistency (and the demon of verification) and the last two are for the benefit of getting the typeset proof into print-ready form.

I started my journey on page one by handing in my notice.

The next step was contained in the last line of the 500-word magazine article, 'The author plans to write a book travelling in the footsteps of Louis MacNeice to be published in 2014 under the pen name of Z W Bates.'

That sign-off line would not change the result of my appointment for the indeterminate area, that appointment was on a date yet to be determined itself, but the sign-off line was a statement that projected beyond.

'The author plans'.

The author, the writer, the company secretary and the lawyer all knew that she could plan all she liked, but if life intervened then there would have to be a new plan.

Still, on a sunlit day in January, the view was of a plan to include Z W Bates and Louis MacNeice and writing.

~

The magazine editor was happy with the prompt and suitable copy received in good time for his printing deadline. I was pleased to have tested, in some small way, the theory that my writing could be something that others might find interesting enough to spend time reading.

As for the indeterminate area, in my head I told myself that for really serious things there would not be so much waiting, but after two doctors put their hand on mine and told me not to worry, my head's rational resolve not to worry, did wobble a bit.

Being English, as I wobbled, I reached for a sporting metaphor. The cricket commentators talk about the corridor of uncertainty: the hard, seamed cricket ball heading down into the place where the batsman is not quite sure whether to put their bat to defend the wicket or perhaps, by putting their bat there, to lose their wicket.

The corridor was poorly lit with uncertainty, but I followed the directions and took the paperwork to the requested place. I waited in the designated area for my appointment. Not quite sure whether the plan I had set myself when I handed in my notice would still be my plan when I left the appointment.

I don't know what this afternoon will bring, I thought.

Yet put like that, it was no different from normal. It was just that the fragility of life had been made visible. Imagination tugged underneath the comfort of today's routine. The gap between now and later widened.

As I walked into the waiting room I saw the afternoon clinic had got off to a bad start. People were everywhere. Like a London mainline railway station when something has gone wrong with the evening rush hour. People in the wrong place, between resigned and exasperated.

And so it came to pass that I went home no clearer. Other things were still to be done. Those things, along with me, were in the pending tray.

I hit the gym for an hour. Heaving at the rowing machine and stamping on the cross-trainer pedals as if they were personally responsible for the untidiness, this interference in the plan for my writing year, for my 12 months as Z W Bates, the author.

I like the order of spreadsheets. I like the tidiness of easily identified cells building into grids with a regular pattern and the preciseness of formulae that do what I tell them to do, until, that is, I try to insert a circular definition.

But to work out where I am, I come back to words. And for the really difficult finding of myself I need a pen and paper, a physical connection between me and the lines that lead me to where I thus discover I am.

In this waiting I heard the Sufi poets say, 'This too shall pass.'

I waited.

It was like my daily commute to work. Better approached in a spirit of watchful neutral. Alert to the unusual, but not something to fight or change. I am in a tunnel between stations. Standing, but with something to read. Operational difficulties, rather than an event as definite as signal failure or as obvious as over-running engineering works. It happens. The commuter can use up energy reacting or save that energy for when they are above the ground and able to use their energy with purpose.

I continued waiting.

One of the things on my To Do list while I waited was to buy a travel-hardy laptop: a tool by which I would create the author writing a Proper Book and also a practical piece of kit for looking things up, making arrangements and keeping in touch. It might (speak it quietly) also be a place for dawdling frivolously in the byways of intriguing factoids and perhaps, even, a place for occasionally idling slowly past irrelevancies.

I stood in my local computer store, projecting myself onto my future writing year. I wanted a keyboard that clicked: 80,000 words is a lot of typing. My technically-minded friends suggested a solid-state drive would be more robust for travelling and made the practical point that I should check the weight of the power cable, as that might negate the weight loss of a smaller-screened laptop.

I looked at the choices. I could demonstrate I had left the corporate world behind for my writing year. I could join the world of the fashionable and buy the badge of the sleekly-moulded in designer white, but even as that thought formed I knew that was not my world.

If a fashionable trend and I ever meet, it is only on a passing intersection, before we both continue on our separate paths. I am a person of words, not pictures, used to the bog-standard word-processing programme, suspicious of the popular (and white shows the dirt too easily).

I decided on a touchscreen laptop. The screen detached to be a tablet. It was resolutely of 2013, so did come with a small risk of being trendy, but it was functional for my purposes. It was encased, not in corporate black, but its near relation, shiny silver.

~

Waiting for my next medical appointment and still feeling in abeyance the following weekend, I took myself off to Margate, a place I had never been, a boundary place on the coast. I was looking for a pending place, a day of sitting on the metaphorical stairs, with no immediate action required.

I left Margate's railway station and set my course along the seafront to the imposed hulk of Turner Contemporary, the new-ish art gallery.

The first room I came to in the Turner gallery had various pieces of wood and metal in it. It had something to offer, but not something easily visible if you were looking for large expanses of Turner's canvases with dramatic sea and cloud. Dozens of plates of sheet metal are not the same.

Unusually the room had two room attendants so I decided not to put either of them on the spot by asking what it was like to stand, and then sit, and then stand again in a dimly-shaded space, with people looking into the space just long enough to see that there were no Turner landscapes there either.

I was expecting a transitional period as I moved from one way of working to another, from the routines of corporate life inked into the diary, to challenges and time-constraints chosen by me; but I had found myself in a different place of transit, in someone else's pending tray. I was adrift in an uncertainty outside the practicalities that I could influence by making conscious decisions.

I left that ill-defined uncertainty to get on with its own thing and pulled myself back to practicalities. In the absence of large-scale Turner landscapes, sweeping sea and land into artistry, I decided to look round the streets of Margate and find some hot food.

There were signs up in Margate's shop windows saying, 'Shut to spring' or some, more positively phrased, 'Open after Easter'. Further on two windswept palms were sturdily trying to bring brighter prospects, even images of the French Riviera, to a salt-misted morning. The palms flanked the doorway of a building that ignored them – named as it was 'The Limes'.

I found a welcoming cafe with an all-day breakfast and good eavesdropping.

'Did he mean to leave her out overnight?', 'Well I would not rely on Picasso'.

I had bought a mug the year before. It was an unnecessary purchase, just for fun, done on impulse, triggered by the message printed on the mug, 'Life is not about waiting for the storm to pass. It's about learning to dance in the rain.' (The near relative of that was, 'You don't enjoy the sunshine if you are always waiting for the storm to come.')

Life needs to include doing some things for fun. Just because. No pretence of worthiness or virtue. Not even a step on a journey. And certainly not a cell in a spreadsheet. Just smelling the roses – well not literally at this time of year, and, with my weak sense of smell, my nose has to be nearly in the bushes for me to smell roses at even the best time of year – savouring the moment. Stirring in the froth of a mug of cappuccino. Seeing if I can still hang a teaspoon from the end of my nose. (It does depend on the depth of the bowl of the particular teaspoon I concluded quite some years ago, but I do like to test my theory from time to time, just to make sure I have not grown up too seriously.)

Doing things for fun is a younger sibling of taking an opportunity. The first opportunity may be the only opportunity. (It may not be, but neither the opportunity nor I will know that when we first meet.) An opportunity may not look like an opportunity. I might be looking pensively at a shut door and the first opportunity might be loitering with an inactive verb. Sometimes it is true that opportunities present themselves, 'Hello, I am an opportunity, with enumerated benefits and in the interests of balance I also self-disclose risks on my reverse.' More often an opportunity and I are not looking for each other, but we somehow fall into conversation, despite the opportunity's bitten finger-nails.

~

And so back to writing; writing as a way of observing myself and creating something that I can then control by editing.

Writing something filled the space of the morning while I waited at the clinic for my next appointment. Waiting where people were doing their jobs, having good days and bad days and days when the computer takes time to load or just does not want to work at all.

We were waiting to have, perhaps our lives changed by people doing their jobs, or perhaps to be given another appointment, or perhaps for life to continue after a semi-colon of waiting; just a pause for uncertainty and then moving on, still in the same paragraph.

I listened to stories of the blue team's meal out last Friday. Who ate what. Who said what. Why someone after all that did not come in the end. As a waiting unit I observed people doing their jobs.

After two hours of being a waiting unit I wondered whether I might have become evidence of, perhaps, a process hiccup.

I am here. My notes are in an unspecified elsewhere. My physical presence does not accord with my status on the computer. I can feel the hardness of the waiting room chair, but I am not sufficiently here. The blue team can see I am here and know I have been waiting over two hours now. The computer can not see that. It knows, with the absolute certainty all computers have, that I am not yet available to be processed.

The clock hand moves on and then a person speaks to another person and, despite the protestations, no doubt, of the computer, both people talk to me and ask me questions and look at me, not the computer. They notice it is my birthday tomorrow. They tell me what will happen next. It does.

I go back to more waiting. Pen in hand I use words to navigate by touch where I find myself.

I knew I was stepping off the known world when I handed in my notice. I knew that while planning is essential, what I planned for and what actually happened, would diverge. And already, here I am, in a divergence.

Four hours on from when the self-service check-in machine refused to recognise me, my file was found and closed. The team agreed that the indeterminate area can be labelled as 'not requiring any workup'. The pictures and notes can go back to be filed, in case reference to my current normal is required in the future.

～

The sunshine outside has the beginnings of warmth in it. I start my birthday early, with another all-day breakfast and a deep cup of mocha this time and, while resuming after my semi-colon of uncertainty, I think of those who did have their lives changed this morning, by people doing their job; while I, I am free to dissolve into an afternoon of idleness and relief, the prologue to my writing year given piquancy by what has not happened today.

2

After the prologue

I had made three lists: a list of the places from MacNeice's life which took my fancy to visit and write about; a list of things that I would not have if I was not in a job; and a list of things to do or think about doing in my writing year.

I clustered the MacNeice places into possible itineraries. I put a balancing column against the things missing without paid employment and I just kept on adding to the third list, the list of things down to me.

One of my working habits was to keep a running list that I called my Forth Bridge List, a list of the things that came into my head that needed doing at some point, or at least needed thinking at some point about perhaps doing at a later point.

Apparently with recent improvements in paint technology, when they get to the end of painting the Forth Bridge they no longer need to start back at the beginning on repainting it, but even if the label is out of date, such a list still works as a conscious parking place. It is a place for things that might, or might not, require a verb to be applied to them in a future timescale: prodding further, actioning, merging one idea with another; now, next week, next month or in the nebulous later.

Putting things on a list clears space in my head for more immediate concerns. Having it all on one list might appear daunting (eight pages later) but it also saves time otherwise spent trying to remember what that passing niggle was behind that half-formed thought. Capturing thought and action, ordering and reordering and then plodding steadily through was what I knew how to do, in cheerful times and in darker times.

Those three lists waited, while I waited, and then I came to the end of the prologue to my writing year and was free to go back to the three lists, back to planning itineraries and thinking about what I might do when I got there.

~

My years of regular business travel had honed my packing list for airport/hotel/meeting room trips. With some effort I had found a piece of luggage that was not the standard black rectangle for those itineraries. It had just enough space for a digressing side trip after those meetings, but as I left the airport after my last business week on the road, my brown roller bag gave up rolling, the outer material ripped and one of the handles was no longer loadbearing.

Then walking through central London in my last week of having an office to go to, the strap of my handbag came away from the body of the bag. It was not for the first time, but I recognised that another repair would be a repair too many. A bag that has all the pockets I have grown used to for all the things that I have needed to carry was not lightly to be cast aside, but there are times when the phrase 'false economy' applies.

I looked at the planned shape of my writing year, without two symbolic pieces of luggage from my past years. While I expected fewer formal handbag days, there would be enough for a new handbag. Looking at my evolving itineraries, wheeled luggage was also going to be called for.

Did I want to replace like with like, locating a direct and functional substitute? Or should I deliberately choose something of another time and place, a new object for a new function?

As to the handbag, I took minimal time in replacing it with another black strapped shoulder bag. No shiny metal buckle. No questioning colour. Plain to the point of invisibility. Fewer compartments than before, but practical in function and not even a second cousin to branded fashion.

The travel luggage took a little longer to locate, not wanting a black rectangle to take with me into my writing year. In the end I settled on a blue, soft-sided case in canvas-like material. It would be visible as an individual, even before I marked its edges with a Z.

～

With my last project completed at work, I took my office suits to the dry cleaners and then came the final handover, the giving back of the work mobile phone.

That phone's all-seeing, red winking eye of wakefulness had told me for years, day in and day out, when it wanted attention. It told me when there was a message waiting to be read, a voicemail to be listened to, an email to be replied to. To be fair to the winking eye, it had often meant that I could do something else,

17

rather than wait by an office phone. As a servant it had many uses. I am old enough to remember staying in the office for phone confirmations and for faxed signatures. But in those receding 1980s once I had that confirmation, that signature, that was it. I left the office and the office did not come with me in the form of a handful of black plastic with a wink.

When I was first issued with the winking eye I did find that part of the menu that allowed me to tell it when to switch off, even if I could not always find that switch for myself. Being mildly non-conformist I set the winking eye shorter winking hours at the weekend, ones I could choose to override, an attempt to put boundaries on the servant/master relationship.

Yet the winking eye was also the badge of a tribe, a tribe from the land of international business where I lived and worked, along with most of my friends. The winking eye told me I was connected and I was a part of a world where I had a place, a role. And then that constant companion was left behind. It was in the office, where I was no longer.

~

The regular asking of what the book was about and why it was MacNeice that I was writing about refined my replies and a reconstruction of those replies was the task for chapter one of *Sunlight*. The weekday alarm went off at my normal weekday time. I took my insulated mug of coffee into my spare room and started typing about why MacNeice and why me.

The central heating went off but the room I was typing in was south-facing so it felt warmer than the rest of the house, as

I discovered when I went downstairs to refresh my coffee. (After two coffees it will be on to herbal teas, I told myself.)

Trying not to be Lot's wife, I did not look back as I typed. I just put down words, following the train of thought. Pruning the over-developed phrase and giving the tangled a good straightening would come later. First I needed to get things down, trap them on paper.

Then I followed my practice from years of minuting meetings. I left my typing to stand, to see what rose and what fell on a later rereading.

I left the house to see some of the daylight I had been writing about. It was wet daylight. I walked to the tube station and then came back a different route, enjoying not entering the tube station at all. The rain stopped. Briefly. Then it started again, more forcefully, with a wintry wind. It made the point that I was outside. On my own. Not connected to the world I had known for so many years. Instead, and knowing no better, I was writing two different books at once.

As a reader I always have more than one book on the go. One for gentle dipping into before I turn out the light at night, one in my briefcase that will not make me laugh out loud (or cry in public) as I travel in and out of central London on public transport and at least one for reading in a comfortable chair downstairs.

So as a writer having two books on the go had a sort of logic. I was more than one writer. There was a writer who researched and attached words to external observations. The sort of writer you might introduce at parties with a business card. Then there was the writer who always wrote, who never went out of the house without a pen and paper, but who rambled, rather than hiked, to a destination.

The hiker might, or might not, be fit enough to complete the route-planned journey. The rambler would go somewhere and then on to somewhere else and wherever that was it would be a journey.

Sunlight is to be about Louis MacNeice and me, travelling and poetry, times and places that are past. It is to be written by a corporate lawyer who is taking a writing year away from corporate life, with structure and discipline and a side helping of fun, just because.

Daylight is this book. It is about writing, about being outside corporate life and what happens along the way, while doing something else. The something else is writing *Sunlight*. What happens along the way will have some structure and discipline but may, I have decided, not be grammatically correct. I will insert full stops where there is no sentence. I will leave some verbs out in the cold and dangle my participles, because I can.

My book, my rules, my writing year.

I will leave terminal prepositions at the end. They work to convey a meaning without telegraphing 'pedant' (up with which I will not put). I might even overlook a split infinitive, but I will watch for my placement of adverbs. I have been in too many US hotel rooms with their coffee machines announcing to me, their target business traveller, 'We proudly brew'.

Adverbs of any type, misplaced or otherwise, are less frequently found in the teens of the 21st century than they were when my use of the English language was being marked at school. Where once the adverb lined up proudly with bold and decisive verbs, maybe even felt itself above the more knockabout adjective, now the adverb waits for any sentence at all to appear in (or even, for any waiting pedant, in which to appear). Maybe the split infinitive will become the last sanctuary of the fading adverb? (To boldly go?)

After my dose of wet daylight, I had bread and cheese for lunch. One of the items in my balancing column of what I thought I would get when not in paid employment, was the opportunity to take my lunch sitting outside, listening to birdsong, feeling warming sunlight.

Reality intruded again. I could sit outside (in a fleece and waterproof), but the birds would be sheltering, not singing, and I would feel the chill of damp, grey daylight, of over-running winter, regardless of the calendar.

I can plan but, as reminded by recent events, there will be a gap between what I might plan and what actually happens. It was T S Eliot who observed 'humankind can not bear too much reality' and yet thinking about that, I am happy not to have advance notice of what I can not do anything about. Not seeing too far into the future is a protective mechanism, a way to avoid facing, head on, too much reality.

One unexpected consequence of putting this writing plan into action is that I have spoken more about myself in the last few months than in the past many years. I know that choosing a writing name is just the start. What attributes will I put on display? Which stories will I tell to a wider audience? Once published, in however few copies, the words will have a life of their own, out there, beyond my control. The words will be interpreted through each reader's own lens of personal experience and they will see things that I do not, things that I might think are not there.

I have been doing a job, which has been my job, but which has not been all of me. We overlap, but we are not one and the same. As with my job, so with my book. I will try not to bristle as I say, 'It is my book, but it is not all of me'.

I have discovered it is not just some people that find what I am doing beyond comprehension. Certain websites are built on the assumption that I must have two different addresses, a work address and a home address. They can not allow me not to have an employer and I simply must have a job title.

I wondered about titling myself 'Experimental Cultural Geographer' but decided that sounded more academic than I am. I toyed with typing in 'Subversive Contrarian (part-time)', enjoying the idea of not being consistent in always taking a contrarily oblique view. Instead I found a phone number to ring up and a live person on the end of the phone who could override the computer's assumption about the shape of my life this coming year.

What I can not find is someone to override the requirement of website programmers for women to choose one of three offered titles. To me the dropdown menu of titles (*Mr*/*Mrs*/*Miss*/*Ms*) serves no useful purpose. It takes up my time but there is no need to distinguish between men with my name and females with my name. Whether I am, or have been married, should be irrelevant for the website, which does not ask that question of men. But that is not the way the website is constructed and ignoring an irrelevant, but mandatory, field is not an option.

I harrumph and move on.

~

Clausewitz, the early 19th century German military strategist, had his concept of the point of main effort when writing about war. For me in this writing year the point of main effort is to write a book (or two) and everything else in my year is to be measured against, or sometimes subordinated to, that.

There is necessary writing, writing for school homework, for university essays, for client updates, for business reports and, on the side, since I was eight or nine, there has always been unnecessary writing, writing for fun, writing for relaxation.

One summer I wrote about a country I had invented, called Damazonia. My guidebook to this imaginary destination had a map of the island and some description of the key topographical features, not that I was precocious enough to call them anything other than hills and rivers. My guidebook did not list any particular rules the people on the island had to abide by; it recorded that those who lived there did their jobs first and then played or read their books for the rest of the day.

A few summers later, going away on a family summer holiday was invented: two weeks on the coast of north Cornwall. I kept a diary for this memorable fortnight and that then grew into a habit. Writing a diary was something I did on holidays.

As a family we often went for a walk. Walking in north Cornwall usually involved me or my sister (who was then shorter than me, being three years younger) being accosted by some ill-mannered brambles or being attacked by a gorse bush when we were on the cliffs above the sandy beaches. On the beaches themselves there was the ever present risk of getting a lump of crude oil stuck to your feet. All the oil we found we attributed to the Torrey Canyon, the supertanker that had hit the Cornish rocks back in 1967.

My holiday diaries were a selective description of events, records of what happened, the truth and nothing but the truth, but not necessarily the whole truth. Once or twice, rereading the written words, I heard the echo of what I did not write. 'I got oil on my feet. Unhappy experience'. We went to another beach later that same day. 'It was horrid. There was not a single rock. All the sand was fluffy. The waves were very big. I have some oil on feet again. Oil, sand, and cold everywhere. Very nasty.' I remember the thick clods of oil being scraped off my feet and the feeling of my feet being scraped off my feet, the raspingly fine sand that got everywhere and stayed there, and the vain search for a reliable rock to sit on, to be a firm base for the scraping.

So I do have a track record of unnecessary writing, writing for fun, writing for relaxation from other writing.

～

My dry-cleaned office suits wait in their plastic covers. I now have no externally-structured routine to put on each morning. I make my own rhythm. I choose pen or keyboard; writing or planning; reading or thinking.

Friends and former colleagues asked if I would blog, have a website, do social media: in short, whether I would come into the

21st century. All of those take time and energy, involve learning a new etiquette and feeding a regular rhythm of updates. I have lived with the pulse of the winking red eye and will do again, but not now. The point of main effort is writing: paragraphs of more than 140 characters and thoughts that can not be illustrated by a tagged picture of me, in jeans and a fleece, sitting at my desk, filling a fountain pen, slowly drawing in black ink and exhaling the phone-free silence.

But the idea of a newsletter takes shape; once every so often, sending out some news in a letter, from the parallel universe I have stepped across into. Some snippets from what I have observed or experienced, edited, as all holiday pictures are (or should be), but representative of the answer to the question of what I have been doing. Not exactly that old standby of school composition, 'What I did on my holidays', but an occasional report from a time away. Not a tweet or a status update, but a sharing from my travelling.

Thinking about what I might share, I allowed myself to be side-tracked by two house sparrows drinking from the puddle on the flat roof beyond my window and then my eye was caught by two fluffed-up birds, two long-tailed tits, flitting excitedly across from fence to washing line and then into the forsythia starting to show yellow just beyond my flat roof.

The pale pink, edged by black, grey and white, of a long-tailed tit is to me evocative. It reminds me of cold winter days with sharp winds forecast (by the long-tailed tits, even if not by weather forecasters), when flocks of 20 or more would scatter through the garden of my childhood as they made their way to more sheltered places.

I have lived in this south London house for 20 years, but I have spent so little daylight here I did not know that the long-tailed tits scattered through this corner of south London too.

Now is that an observation to be shared, an illustration in more visible form of what I have discovered, that I am now able to see things that were always here.

Or is it an over-sharing?

~

My local tube station is on the Northern Line, a tentacle of the London underground that reaches into south London and is coloured black on the tube map. This week there is a poster on the northbound platform, for holidays in Texas. 'Let your inner cowboy run wild'. I am not sure about my inner cowboy, or indeed about me, running wild, but in south London I am preparing to take myself off to Texas. For my first trip of my writing year I have given myself two weeks in the reading room of the Harry Ransom Humanities Research Center in the University of Texas in Austin, where the largest number of MacNeice's manuscripts are. They are accessible to someone like me, with photo ID but nothing more. No accreditation from a post-graduate course. No validation from a string of post-nominal letters. Just a curious individual.

I am into my second week of looking out into the daylight as I type. The puddle on my flat roof is frozen hard this morning.

In my writing room there are three bookcases; a desk, self-assembled from flat pack; a clip-on desk light; a self-assembled, leather-look chair and a second chair for no particular purpose, a daydreaming chair. The newest addition to the room's furniture is a cardboard box that I have slotted with dividers, while I evolve a filing system for my notes, the oddments of MacNeice I capture in my reading in preparation for my travels.

At the moment the categorisation of the dividers is by place and the order of the dividers is according to my draft timetable. Between each divider is a wallet with jottings of riffs that I might play in the chapter on that place and, more prosaically, a timetable or costing for travelling to that place this year. I also have the first draft of my own style sheet, answering the question of whether to call the country the US (with or without dots), the USA (ditto) or America. I have a ready-made, starter list of places where inconsistency may contradict itself, places that I have been sensitized to over my years of annual reports and now I have the luxury of writing my own book I can hyphenate (or not) ready-made as I please.

~

One of the older books (inherited from my lay-preaching grandfather via my aunt) in my largest bookcase is a slim volume of G K Chesterton's *Selected Essays*, which I took commuting with me, despite it making me both laugh and cry. One of the essays was about leisure and the different types of leisure. One type of leisure was the time to do something other than paid work, though what that might be could be as narrowly prescribed as some paid work is. A second type of leisure was the time to do anything, with anything having no starting definition and being much rarer than we might at first think, a time of creation without prescription. The third type of leisure was time doing nothing.

Chesterton was of the view that leisure was not the same as liberty. Doing something in a certain way, as expected by you or by those around you, was not liberty and doing nothing was certainly not liberty. Leisure to create whatever you chose to was liberty for Chesterton (at least in that essay).

I am at liberty in Chesterton's second type of leisure. Free to create whatever I choose.

Reading Chesterton's essay took me back to my 18-year old self, with a summer job on the shop floor of a caster wheel factory, analysing the different categories of boredom (as I sealed the required number of screws and washers into plastic bags one day and then boxed up 100 sets of four caster wheels and their attendant bag of screws and washers the next, each set ready to go on the foot of a TV stand in the days when TVs were many-sided and bulky).

I never quite concluded my definitive list of boredom categories, nor their ranking in order of destructiveness and, each time I revisited the memory, the list slipped into a different shape.

That list of types of boredom went something like this:

~ Doing something that is not what you want to do beyond the summer, but is a means to an end. Even as I was failing to be much help in finishing the communal word puzzle in the canteen's coffee break magazine I knew I was learning, so it did not qualify as boring.

~ Doing something that is not what you want to do because it takes you away from where you want to go, moving you away from your planned end. My 18-

year old self resolved never to go there, a place where boredom shrivelled what a person had been or might be and where grew a festering resentment of 'could have' or 'should have'.

~ Repetitive actions that leave your mind free (to do such things as analyse the categories of boredom).

~ Repetitive actions which need some degree of concentration (so you forget whether you have delineated three or four categories of boredom so far and fail to spot which of the categories might overlap in part).

~ Repetitive actions which, if you do not concentrate, could lose you your finger. That was the boredom that made the exact length of each coffee and lunch break critical. That was the boredom that made sense of the news stories about trade union strikes over who did what when. That was the boredom of body and spirit and after a day of that I needed, not the leisure of doing nothing, but to do something (prescribed or otherwise). Though to be fair to the memory of that caster wheel factory, we did all rotate round the jobs, with no more than one day at a time in any one category, varying our types of boredom.

So here I now am, many years on from that factory summer job, doing what I have decided I want to do for a year. The point of main effort, the writing, has many constituent parts and I know there will be times (in the plural) when the phrase 'It seemed like a good idea at the time' will come to mind.

~

There is a forecast of thunderstorms followed by temperatures up into proper summer degrees in Austin, Texas, by the time I get there next week.

The BBC website can do many things, but it has no easy answer to my question about the weather to be found in the middle of the north Atlantic in several weeks' time. For that is my next destination. After my two quiet study weeks in the Harry Ransom Humanities Research Center of the University of Texas, Austin I plan to come home from the US by sea and therefore on a containership.

Yes, I agree that *therefore* is perhaps misplaced. There are ships other than containerships that come across the Atlantic. Just because I fancy travelling by sea there is no *therefore* that says I must travel by containership, but there are some things to be done this year Just Because and a containership voyage is one of them. It is something I have fancied doing since my first job as a lawyer, buying and selling ships. It has a MacNeice link, albeit a tenuous one. His trips to the US in 1939 and 1940 were by sea. Ten days on the high seas on a containership is not the same as passage on a scheduled liner such as the *Queen Mary* and, when I come to leave my landlocked hotel room in North Carolina for the north Atlantic, even in May, a containership voyage may very well come into the category of 'It seemed like a good idea at the time'.

~

April. The clocks had gone forward to British Summer Time, but the thermometer had not been paying attention and remained firmly at the winter end of the scale. The generous warmings of sunshine for the day before my birthday that enthused the daffodils and crocuses have been cut back by a sharp wind and the attendant absorbing greyness has taken away that promise of spring daylight.

Snow blew across my garden as I engaged in the feat of imagination that was packing for Austin, Texas and the north Atlantic. I started with the easy accessories: sunglasses and waterproofs; adaptor plugs for the US and for the German-flagged vessel some continental European adaptor plugs; an alarm clock and a windup torch.

One lesson from my business travels over the years has been that the light switch, or card holder to operate the whole lighting system, may well not be obvious when you first enter the hotel room and is unlikely to be easy to operate from the bedside. Hence I take a windup torch (to avoid another bruising encounter with a piece of furniture on the way to a master switch in a foreign room).

Packing wisdom handed on to me years ago was to include a sarong (taking up little space but covering a multitude of potential functions, particularly when sleeping and washing arrangements were not as they might be) and a scarf (of the decorative sort, ready to unexpectedly dress up for any best silver and cut-crystal dinner that might materialise). I thought of the fierce air-conditioning of Texas and added some long sleeves before I overdosed on.Tshirts. I remembered a working ship that I travelled on years ago and took multiple layers. I assumed laundry once a week, and then added some extras for the flexing of that assumption.

I have a list of things to do the Day Before Leaving and none of them can be done any sooner without having to be undone and redone. I mark off each item, consciously, a checklist, with comforting marks, that shows me what I have done. The alternative is my subconscious getting on with all the jobs and then not 'knowing' whether I just thought 'I must unplug the radio alarm' or whether I did actually do it.

Last Night Nerves.

In 1997 I spent a week on a tall ship in Vanuatu. In 2001 I had two weeks at sea coming from St Helena to the UK on a mail ship. Both trips involved ports of call that (in pre-internet search engine days) tested a good atlas. The day before I left for each trip (and indeed many others) I wondered why it had seemed a good idea to venture so far away from the heard of. I have never been seasick, but the prospect of a first time swells in front of me. I am happy with my own company, but I know that for the five weeks of this trip I will have met no one before. I will be a stranger among people focused on their own day job to be done. I will be a name (I hope) on their list. So tonight, hanging round each light switch are a myriad uncertainties. Uncertainties I have chosen to inflict on myself.

Once I have crossed my threshold and locked my front door I will be fine. I too will believe what I have been telling people. Some dreams are just that, nice to have, to look at from time to time, to drift into fluffily for a bit of light relief from the world. And some dreams are ones to go after.

So I am ripping aside the idling, dawdling thought of 'sometime I might see if I can write a book' and setting out with my laptop and a rolling programme of uncertainties, leaving my routines and my backstory behind. Even as I do that, I know that in going after a dream I may lose it all together and that sharpens the edge on my Last Night Nerves.

I do not remember who it was that said, 'You miss 100% of the shots you don't take'. A confident, basketball-playing American perhaps? I am not at all sure that the record of shots I do take will be so much better than the record of those I don't take, but I tell myself it is indeed time to take some shots.

I make supper of the remnants from my fridge, throwing out things that will have turned green or blue in five weeks, leaving eggs, butter, lemon juice and cider to greet my return. When faced with uncertainty I reach for the security blanket of a list, so I make a food shopping list for my return and tuck that under one of the magnets on my fridge door.

3

April on the road
with MacNeice

I had a daytime flight to the US, landing in Chicago and then on to Austin.

I had a window seat and this time I had no work to do on the flight, no stash of reading to get through, no meetings to prepare for and at the other end there would be no person with my name on a board to meet me.

I had a row of seats to myself as there was only a light scattering of passengers in Economy, while Business Class was full of keyboards, faces glowing a faded blue from the halflight of laptop screens.

Somewhere over Greenland or northern Canada, I reached for my camera as the cloud cleared onto unedited whiteness. Then the blank canvas fissured into black fingers of river. I took several pictures of uninhabited vastness, sculptured snow and ice far below, a reminder of what happened to be passing, when I looked out of the window, when I was no longer nose down into a task to be completed by the time I landed.

By the time I did land Chicago had had weather with a capital

W and the departures board had turned yellow with delays. Austin was one of the connection cities called out before I even got off the plane. I dutifully identified myself to ground staff and was handed a magic card. I waved my card and lo, a never-before occurrence, a new immigration desk opened just for me, well for six of us aliens, to be processed so we could make our connections.

That assumed that our connections were ready for us, which in my case, was not the case. My onward flight was delayed by 2½ hours. Nothing turned on it. No one was waiting for me in Austin. I only needed to arrive in time to have a night's sleep before I registered at the 'HRC', the Humanities Research Center, at the University.

I can just be. Sitting in transit. Looking out at what happens to be passing.

On a business trip nearly 20 years ago I found myself with more than five hours to wait at Moscow's domestic airport terminal. Something I do not recommend. The experience comes back to me whenever I am handed down some unplanned transit time. Ways of being in the neutrality of transit that work for me are:

1   Making a list or three: a way of controlling that which
    I can control, and of projecting myself into another
    time, the time beyond waiting, with my travel luxury
    which is also my travel essential, namely a pen and
    some paper.

2   Speculating (internally, within the safety of several
    brackets and caveats) about the people around me: this,
    in some countries, is better done by concentrating

on the feet and footwear of those around, rather than looking at the whole person, running the risk of offending, or worse, and triggering consequences from eye contact.

3   Finding a noticeboard with small print to read, to tell me things that the big, bold posters will not. If the language is not English I may have to retreat to making anagrams of the letters I can see, which, in an airport full of Cyrillic in the early 1990s, left me with very little to read.

Chicago in 2013 gave me many possibilities to indulge in all three transit activities. I watched a table of 20-somethings eating, while operating at least one electronic device each. One was bantering with a physically present friend, with an earphone playing something else into his ear. Another was chatting on her phone, while sending messages on her tablet, perhaps to the person on the phone.

I too had a veritable undergrowth of cables in my hand luggage: one charger for my laptop, another for my digital camera, a connecting cable for my MP3 player to play me sounds of home (or their proxy, being podcasts from the BBC website) and a charger for my e-book reader, and that was before the 'just in case' mobile and its charger buried at the bottom of the entanglement.

～

Later that evening the taxi from the airport pulled up at the address I gave the driver, the address of the bed and breakfast I had booked for my two weeks in Austin. I had picked out from the internet that particular B&B as being near to a bus route to the university campus, always having someone sleeping there overnight and having a communal breakfast table. It was a yellow, two-storey house, where two roads in a residential neighbourhood crossed.

There was no one around. There were no sounds as I opened the car door. I paid and the cab pulled away. On the plus side, it was still daylight.

Much though I bristled in the past when the doorman at one of the chain name hotels wanted, before I had got out of the cab, to take my business trip luggage, on arrival there I had always known I was in the right place. Familiar branded logos told me what I could expect. Here the house did not have a name plate visible.

My email confirmation said to go to the side door. For a few moments on the crossroads I was not even sure which door would be described as the side door.

~

At breakfast the next morning a group of retired friends from central Florida were going to do the Lyndon Johnson presidential library and the LBJ ranch, swing by Fredericksburg and maybe a few other places where the influence of German settlers was still visible, pop into the wildflower centre on the way home and then find a place for some live music. A programme so they could say that they had seen this part of Texas.

Also at breakfast were a couple of horticulturalists from Chicago and they were planning a whole day, at least, maybe two, at the wildflower centre.

And me? I admitted to coming to Austin to read manuscripts in a library on the university campus. I said it was a holiday treat to myself. One of the horticulturalists was very interested in the writings of John Clare, a poet of 19th century Northamptonshire, so he could understand the idea of following a poet onto another continent, just out of interest, just because. From the crevices where odd-shaped facts linger, I pulled out enough about John Clare to build something of a conversation on the subject.

It seemed easier for the purposes of exchanging breakfast conversation to leave out my thinking of writing a book and having a year away from paid employment. The breakfast table guessed, from my accent, that I was Australian, so I did also admit to coming from London. We agreed around the table that, if in doubt, it is better to guess Australian than to tell a South African or New Zealander that you think they are from London.

~

A description that lodged with me from speaking to someone more travelled than me many years ago, was that good travelling showed you 'other people's normal'. Going to the grocery store to buy a weekly bus pass did that.

I wanted to buy a bus pass, not only to save money over the course of my two weeks in Austin, but also to save the hassle of conserving a ready supply of unwrinkled one dollar bills for each bus fare.

The phrase 'grocery store' had conveyed to me an image of a small shop on a street corner, so I was surprised when my directions led me to a huge warehouse hangar. I then walked most of the way round it looking for the entrance. A sign in a window set out the subsection of legislation which meant that, in one store at least, concealed hand guns were not permitted, reminding me that in so many other places they were permitted and also reminding me that Austin was very much in Texas.

Once inside the store I asked for some more help with directions. 'You need the Business Center.' It seemed a grand term for a place to buy a bus pass. I bought two, one for each week of being a student of Louis MacNeice in Austin and set off again across the car park, across the entire continent that is an American parking lot. It demonstrated to me, from a small and crowded country, how 'big' is the default option in the vastness that is the US.

I wondered about that vastness again when at lunch I came across a bottomless cup, a cup that can be refilled time and time again for no extra charge in the land of potentially limitless consumption.

My table neighbours on one side that lunchtime were students in animated discussion about whether a relationship had become a habit. I hoped, for the sake of the unnamed 'she', that this was a discussion about characters in a TV series, not about friends of theirs.

Across from me, piercing through the student chatter, was a severely enunciated, female voice on a mobile phone, 'No, this is his ex-wife who is calling.' The emphasis was heavily on the ex. The gatekeeper on the other end of the call must have got a bad case of crossed wives.

~

'My' B&B was an Historic Lodging, built in 1911, a few years after my home in south London, so I was staying in a house that creaked comfortably, much like home. For some of the guests it was a thing of wonder to stay in such an old house, but for all of us it meant that not all the angles were right angles and some of the horizontals were not entirely perpendicular to their nearest verticals.

I got into a rhythm of coming down for breakfast at 8 o'clock and joining whatever conversation the table might have to offer between strong coffee, home-made granola, yogurt and whatever B&B host Eric was cooking, which often required a translation for me. Blueberry muffins and cinnamon rolls needed no translation, but eggs with things in them were less obvious to me.

I tried, but concluded black beans, even if not refried, were not for me at breakfast. Later in the day I might be able to manage them; no promises though - lunch might still be too early for their softened lumpiness that I had not grown up with.

One fellow guest introduced herself as being from Houston, Texas. I introduced myself as from London, England. After we had exchanged a few more sentences she remarked that I had very good English. I did wonder what language she thought would be my mother tongue, but decided not to ask.

Some days the chairs in the main room downstairs gave seats to people moving efficiently from point A to point B. We smiled, perhaps said 'hello', had breakfast at the same table and moved on. Some days the fellow guests were more loquacious, but my being from London was too foreign, too difficult before the first coffee of the morning, so it was easier to keep to Texan topics of conversation. Most days the breakfast conversation took a turn somewhere of interest, perhaps to places seen or to see. Or perhaps to places not to bother seeing. I was glad I had chosen to ensure that, without trying, I always had some conversation, before I settled myself in for five or six hours of gently reading manuscripts, quietly immersing myself in another world, distant in place and getting more distant in time.

~

For my mid-day break from the reading room I walked through the campus past the various recruiting tables laid out in the shade of a designated place. The Caribbean Students' Association had music pumping and was running a competition involving gyrating hula-hoops. The Republican Students at the next table could not compete.

Burnt orange, the colour of the University of Texas, was everywhere. The motif of their football team, the Longhorns, was on everything I might have imagined it would be on and quite a few things I could not have imagined until I looked in at the three (yes three) floors of their shop. UT could be put on anything. How about an artificial Christmas tree in burnt orange and white or a onesie (the 2013 craze for all-in-one romper suits for adults) in burnt orange and white? There were sweatshirts and shorts of all sizes and shapes, with racks of Tshirts that would be too large as a dress on me. There were also some items of clothing that did not have enough material to deserve a whole name to themselves.

As a student in England I went to a university where the

one thing you knew was that someone in a sweatshirt with the university's name emblazoned in capitals across their front, was not a matriculated member of that university. If you looked closely at a student's sports bag or their casual top or even, after they had graduated, a car sticker, their university's name might be there, but never in chest-high, five-inch letters, that could glow in the dark.

Each day as I walked from my campus bus stop to the reading room and back, I counted the ratio of burnt orange items to students. I never seemed to count up to more than ten people before I also saw someone in UT burnt orange. One of the burnt orange tops I saw regularly as I walked through campus in April 2013 proclaimed 'Class of 2016'. The confidence of the announcement. The assumption of graduation.

One day a sign went up to alert drivers to 'High Pedestrian Activity'. Was that like a pollen count? Pedestrian activity levels rise as the weather gets more suitable and US drivers need to be warned about such unusual phenomena as people walking? It might cause irritation or worse? Still the motorists could take comfort that it would not last. Austin may jog, cycle and skateboard in the spring. It may walk itself and its dogs in the freshness of April but soaring summer temperatures will send people back into their air-conditioning before June.

～

The Humanities Research Center was shut on Sundays and Saturday afternoons, but I had already decided that I would have a full two days for my weekends in Austin and I would play the tourist, albeit the slightly peculiar tourist with a bus pass, not a rental car.

Tourist day one I decided the thing to see was the LBJ library. It was on the UT campus so I found my way there easily on the tried and trusted number 7 bus. At the library's entrance they wanted to know my zip code and the computer could not cope with my having a London post code instead. The computer could cope with my not having a car and so not having any parking to validate.

My formal learning of history took me as far as England under the Tudors, so I admit my timeline of American history is sketchy, but the Vietnam war and the Civil Rights era are broader than just being American history and I enjoyed the displays (and getting distracted by some of the footwear of my fellow visitors).

The sculpture garden was said by a notice to be closed due to the inclement weather. The weather was as clement as anyone could wish for as I walked away from the LBJ library and back down to the bus stop. Now the idea was to take the bus I knew, the number 7, to the bridge over what is the Colorado River, dammed at that point into a lake, the Lady Bird Lake (which sounds better than its previous name of Town Lake) and then change to a new bus to head south to the lively, new home of Austin happening, South Congress.

As the bus swung sharply out to the east I realised I should have got off the bus just before we crossed the bridge, not waited until we were accelerating over a flyover, through a turning for the junction with I-35 (which I knew was off the edge of the tourist map deep within my bag), down to traffic lights where men were holding up cardboard signs, past gas stations three-quarters shut.

Two options came to mind. First option: stay on the bus until the end of the route and then come back again. The first problem with the first option was bus stations are not usually places to hang around. Second option: since this was now back to being a two-way road, get off at the next stop, nip across the road and hope I do not have to wait too long for the salvation of a number 7 bus coming in the other direction, back to downtown.

Peering ahead to the next bus stop, I saw it had a small huddle of shops around it. They looked more tended. I opted for option two and decided not to find out where bus number 7 went next with its cargo of oddly silent Hispanic family groups.

Option two came in three parts. Part one was easy enough. I made the decision and I got off. Part two was the nipping across the road part. That was easier said than executed. It was a two-way road, but each direction had three lanes. I concentrated on one way at a time. The median, the central reservation, was wide enough to give me pause for breath before I scuttled over the other section of road and up to the shade of the bus shelter for the stop in the other direction.

Moments later a bus with a new number pulled up. It was not the safety of the known number 7. I considered whether this might be a frying pan taking me into the fire but persuaded myself I had seen the number 20 on bus stops in downtown, so I got on and happily it swiftly performed part three of option two and took me back to downtown where I should have got off the original number 7 in the first place.

Now if I was a proper Traveller I would not have got on the wrong bus or, if I did, I would have travelled to the end of the route and found a whole new world to tell my readers about, something to heighten a contrast with the worlds of staying in a neighbourhood B&B and trawling MacNeice manuscripts from the 1940s and 1950s.

However I am not a proper traveller with a capital T, just me, mildly given to curiosity that is strong enough to take me to Austin and get me on a bus in the first place, but weak enough that I am thankful to have got back to my starting point without a memorable story to tell, and indeed nothing to pay for my mistake because of the benefit of a bus pass.

The next bus to South Congress was crowded. I got on, shuffled down the bus and a seated passenger asked if I knew where a certain intersection was. Do I look like I know anything? Me. The one who just got off the wrong bus. Or is it that I have an approachable face? I shuffled back to the front again and asked the driver, but he did not know anything I could usefully relay to the seated passenger.

~

I got off the bus on South Congress and went inside a snack bar with the self-evident name *Snack Bar*. In fact what they served was more than a snack; there were proper meals, with a fine array of people-watching thrown in as a side order. The menu offered flash-fried Brussels sprouts, but my bus journeys had taken me far enough out of my comfort zone for one day, I opted for French fries with my steak sandwich. I added further to my day's sightings of dramatic boots: a red leather pair with ornate stitching, a dark brown pair shone to rival mirrors and a toddler asleep on his father's shoulder with Cuban-heeled, two-tone leather boots.

'Do you want me to box the fries?' I heard the words, but they did not come attached to any comprehensible meaning. I concentrated and had a fleeting vision of an unequal contest between my cold potatoes and the rippling muscles of my waiter, whom I could quite believe to be a boxer in his time off. Even when, belatedly, the sense of the words did arrive, the concept of anyone taking cold potatoes for a walk round the shops and then home was foreign.

'No thank you, just the check'. I had at least got used to not confusing matters by asking for the bill at the end of the meal. There was a whole chain of possible confusion twisting in wait, as the British bill would be paid using notes, while the same action would be an American check being paid using bills.

After my meal and some restoration of post-bus journey equilibrium, I went on to browse in wonderment in a boot shop. I had left a pair of boots in south London, which there verge on the flamboyant, but in that Austin boot shop would have been shrinking violets. My boots are just one colour and that colour is a homely brown. They have some stitching, but that too is brown. In front of me were racks of boots, three or more colours of leather each, stitched in abstract patterns or cut by exact design into a specified emblem. The racks went from floor to just below the ceiling. The boots were sorted by size, but were mostly mid-calf in length. They paraded through the store, a glorious range of embroidered leatherwork.

When I first went into the store it was with the idea of buying a leather belt, but even the buckles in there did not pass the 'could

I really wear that in south London' test. I marvelled. I even took some photos, but while the more abstract 'one' might be able to wear such a belt on the Northern Line, the more specific 'I' that is me, even the me that is writing a book or two, could not and so I left without making a purchase.

Over the road was a hat shop. Not a 'ten-gallon, we went to Texas to see cowboys' hat shop, but a shop run and staffed by people who liked hats. I lingered there, among the straw hats, with care and cleaning instructions prominently displayed, between the many shades of trilbys and fedoras. A mother and daughter were nearly dissolved into utterly helpless laughter while trying on big-brimmed floppy hats. There was a deep blue, felt hat that might, perhaps, on a confident day, have passed the 'could I really wear that in south London' test, but it would have been a close call. Knowing the shape of my luggage and the nature of my journey to come I left the hat unbought.

The noise from the matinee show at the Continental Club strode out on to the street as its heavy door opened to let customers in and out from their smoking breaks. I went in and got my hand stamped, with a cross bones and a skull wearing a rather bouffant soft cap. The people in the hat shop would no doubt have had a proper name for that cap.

The Club looked gloomy on entering. It had a bar down the left-hand side and, at right angles, six rows of high chairs looking out onto the entertainment. A man was twanging a guitar thickly. A lady was quietly minding her own business on keyboards and then, when given the nod from time to time, she unleashed a strikingly different voice. Drums and another guitar added to the mix of country-style music, overlaid with lyrics of heartache after unsubstantiated optimism.

The room was overseen by a glittering mirror ball in the ceiling, rotating slowly over an impressive collection of dancers doing 'proper' dancing. They made up a kaleidoscope of pairs in unlikely mixtures of shapes and sizes, but each pair avoided the others on what was a small dance floor. They added to my collection of observed cowboy boots, as did the band, brightly lit on a small stage. No room for major striding to and fro on that stage. One pace forward and back. Perhaps, if your fellow band members knew what was coming and had time to get out of the way, one pace side to side.

Despite the size of the room, the man sitting on a raised perch at the back, with an array of sliding controls, appeared to be taking the decision to slide a control fractionally up or down, based on what he could see through a pair of binoculars.

There was a big barrel of water on the edge of the bar that the dancers visited between partners, for there was plenty of changing of partners. I could not work out whether they were all Saturday afternoon regulars who knew each other or out-of-towners who knew the received etiquette about partner-swapping. The dancers came from each decade, including ladies in their 70s who swirled their skirts up, one to a level of almost complete revelation.

~

Despite repeated soapings, the Continental Club's skull and cross bones were still on the back of my hand when a large A was stamped across them. I had gone to have a look round the Austin

Arts Festival, where I found I got free entry, by virtue of my having a bus pass, not a car.

The roads around City Hall were shut for the weekend event and I perched on the steps of City Hall, under dappled shade, enjoying the warm breeze, while a band of four girls and a boy played their set. The boy on a guitar was an accident waiting to happen, his electric guitar cable went one way as his red trainers pranced another. The drums and first keyboard swopped smiles and instruments. The second keyboard and a second guitar looked very self-contained in their worlds. Then the boy took to vocals and the overall effect deteriorated for me, though the toddler, with his dad on the steps in front of me, continued clapping along.

I pottered off to look at the artwork, displayed for sale in tented stalls. I had my regular temptation of whether to buy some polished wood items, but resisted that more easily than some wall hangings made by a former teacher of English who melted glass onto pieces of steel and copper, themselves soldered together from mostly rectangular oddments. Putting unlikely things together in unlikely ways appealed to me, but while I might have found a place in my house for 18 inches of glass and metal, I knew such an addition to my baggage would not fit into my suitcase.

I wandered on through the stalls of more usual art fair things, or so I thought, looking at a landscape painting which on closer examination was in fact an embroidery. A little further on clothes were draped over hangers hooked up on nails at the back of a stall and when I got closer I saw the effect was achieved with metalwork.

I overheard one painter, 'Yep I moved to Chicago 'cos paint just doesn't dry in Houston.' There were practicalities to take into account in all walks of life.

The next stall I stopped at had quite a crowd around it and was selling cutting boards and coasters, decorated with a range of images from in and around Austin. I nearly succumbed to a coaster with a picture of an older manhole cover, the unnecessarily decorative ironwork having caught my eye as it did the eye of the photographer. The prices displayed were simple round figures, which meant the lady manning the stall was in constant danger of running out of change as the prices, once tax had been added, were distinctly not round. (The US is a country where the displayed price is not the price that you pay. The various applicable sales taxes get added on afterwards.) She also had the further complication of the City of Austin having recently introduced a ban on 'single-use plastic bags' which was news to most of her customers who were just visiting Austin for the day. She had to explain why she could not be helpful and give them a bag to put their purchases in as they walked round the rest of the fair.

And then I was back at the City Hall, with another band warming up. The lead singer this time was female, dressed in black and white: black and white top, black trousers and then black and white stripped wellington boots, which, as the temperature headed into the territory I label as properly hot, must have been very uncomfortable. Suffering for your art?

~

Austin has a mantra of 'Keep Austin Weird', which I first read as wired and then doubted that the city would have the sort of technology problems that risked unplugging the whole place. On closer examination, some of the weirdness of Austin would seem unremarkable in London; but some of it was aggressively self-conscious, a 'look at me' declaration. The better parts of the weirdness were just people being themselves, regardless of who was looking or what others might think.

For some Texans it might be weird for a meat-eater to have a meal at a vegetarian restaurant. For me (although a carnivore) it was a tasty and good value choice from the many on the well-populated restaurant junction, an evening stroll from my B&B. The restaurant had confidence in its vegetables. It was not one of these veggie hangouts that had a menu full of tofu pretending to be chicken or lentils clubbing together in the hope of passing themselves off as meat.

The harpist was an unusual touch, but live music in all its variety was diversity to be celebrated – and maybe that counted as Weirdness for people who live within a definition of normal that is lined with an impermeable membrane of uniformity.

On my second tourist weekend I went to one of the areas discussed over the B&B's breakfast table. I got my bus stops right and uneventfully reached the intersection of Lamar and 6th. First I went into an independent book shop, laid out with categories that I recognised, though their placement no doubt reflected their customer base. The Business and Management category was cheek by jowl with Teen Lit and further away from the front door than it might be in other cities (if, that is, you could find a bookshop anymore in the downtown of many other US cities). So what did I not buy there? An oversized Tshirt with the legend 'With enough thrust pigs fly just fine' and a book entitled *The Glamor of Grammar.*

Second stop was an independent record shop with racks full of physical vinyl records and CDs, things to browse and thereby find what you were not looking for, thanks to serendipity, not a computer algorithm. The basic layout was alphabetical by name of artist, which put musicians next to each other regardless of their style of music and had the same effect on the browsing customer. New and used records were also put in together, on the entirely reasonable assumption that the customers of that shop were looking for music they wanted to listen to, not shiny new purchases to display.

Making my way through the alphabet I suddenly realised I had strayed. It was Record Store Day and independent record shops were holding events, musicians playing live and then signing records. In my idling along the racks I had queue-jumped a line of men in beards and/or black Tshirts, clutching LP album covers and waiting for a fellow beard in black Tshirt to sign them. I apologised in my best English voice to the bouncer and asked if he could let me past his rope and point me in the direction of S, which he did with a very pleasant smile, a reminder to me that I should not jump to conclusions when I see an armful of tattoos.

There was a section to one side of the shop for compilations, which was then ordered by music style, with each subsection separated by a rigid plastic divider, labelled at the top. I enjoyed the honesty of one such label, 'Various Hard to Classify World Music Artists'.

The joy of browsing book or record shops was perhaps already one lost to those who live in the 21st century. No doubt it will be superseded by joys that my sister's children in a few years' time will despair of trying to explain to their aunt from the 20th century.

Since CDs are small and light and the used CDs were scarcely the price of a branded coffee I did buy some country music CDs and a CD from Chicago (the band).

During the week I had looked up who was playing at a bus route-friendly venue. (Even for me the 21st century's internet has plenty of uses.) Chicago were at the ACL Live venue at the Moody Theatre so I went along. The theatre had a capacity of 2,750, spread across three levels, but even in my cheaper seat I could almost see the sweat glistening on the performers. Only two of the band were wearing white shirts, the rest were in black, which under the lights put me in mind of the impracticality of the lead singer in wellington boots at the Austin Arts Fair. My fellow audience members were more in sandals and trainers than cowboy boots. (I began to understand the number of pedicures advertised.) One mother and daughter made their way down the steps in front of me, carefully defying the laws of physics in their four-inch tottering heels. A wife unable to locate her glasses handed over the tickets and asked her already-bespectacled husband to read out the seat numbers.

The show had changes of lighting and changes of tempo, but no smoke and mirrors to distract the audience from the point of main effort, the music. From my seat I could see the stage hands lining up the various instruments to bring up on stage for the band. The trombonist was quite a showman, hamming up his playing in a rock band, and then, when I had just about got used to the idea of a rock trombonist, the saxophone player was handed a flute, which seemed an awkward thing to play while still hanging a saxophone round your neck, but musically worked.

So memories of a good evening lead me to buy the Chicago CD. The lady on the cash desk (pierced and tattooed beyond the levels I was getting used to) asked if I had found what I was looking for, to which I had in truth to reply I was buying things I had not come in to the shop to look for.

That evening I went to another concert. Again something I had not been looking for, but passing by the Paramount Theatre I saw the advertised Saturday evening show was a jazz pianist whose name I vaguely recognised, playing with someone I had never heard of, but, given the depth of my ignorance about jazz, was no doubt famous in his own right too. The balcony tickets still available combined a good price with, being on the left-hand side, a good view of the pianist's hands. The seats were velvet-covered and with none of the cup-holders the Chicago audience had. The theatre was in the style of a London West End theatre, except the boxes (not being sold for this performance) were facing forward, looking at the stage, not looking out over the audience as they do in London. The stage seemed not very deep. It was framed by a proscenium arch. There was ornate plasterwork on the ceiling and high above the stage was an angel playing a harp one-handedly, waving to her public with the other hand. Was she daring to mime to a soundtrack in this, the town that prides itself on live music? From where I was sitting it seemed as though the harp-playing angel had also concussed with her wings a rather crumpled-looking angel, lying on the floor behind her. Was she so busy waving to her public she had not been in full control of both wings?

My seat neighbour was into his jazz. His reason for coming to the concert was Brad Mehldau. Although I had seen the Brad Mehldau Trio play, I could not remember when or where that concert was, so I was unable to keep my end up in the conversation. Both of us knew as little about Chris Thile, though my seat neighbour had the advantage of having seen a mandolin before and he knew where Nashville was.

A younger couple two rows in front provided distraction. She was wearing a dress that appeared to have bat wings attached. I was idly wondering about her apparent wings, when she gave her phone to her partner. He unzipped the top of the bat wing, just under her hairline, exposing a startlingly red interior to what was now revealed to be, functionally, a jacket pocket, though positioned so the wearer needed a friend they were really quite friendly with, before they could use the space as a pocket.

The theatre manager came on stage to thank all the sponsors and introduce the introducer. The introducer came on stage to introduce Brad Mehldau and Chris Thile. Only then could the concert begin.

The jazz pianist Brad was weaving in and out of the bluegrass of Chris on the mandolin, which seemed a cramped sort of instrument to play, strung round his neck like a guitar, but on a much shorter cord. Brad, greying quietly in velvet jacket and urban sneakers, left the younger man to sing and to introduce the songs. Chris in jeans and cowboy boots, mixed his heavy twanging with some gentle strumming. When he really got going he looked like a puppet attached to invisible strings, kicking out a leg or pulling up his head. We did hit a pick, pick, picking repetitive section on the mandolin when I fell to wondering how female players angled their mandolin to play? Or did they, more sensibly, lengthen the neck cord? That section passed and the 90-minute set flowed enjoyably on to the one allotted encore, before the lights went up and there was no doubting that the show was over.

Out at the bus stop, still waiting for the number 7 bus, I bumped into fellow B&B guests, a couple from Calgary who were in Austin for the MotoGP, the grand prix for motorcycles. I described how I had seen a pack of perhaps 20 Harley-Davidsons being shepherded through downtown that morning by a police escort that seemed to be holding the traffic lights for them. Mr Calgary was obviously not in favour of Harley-Davidsons.

Mrs Calgary and I continued some of our earlier breakfast conversation about what we were each doing in Austin. Talking to her there was less risk of tripping over embedded assumptions than there was with some of the B&B guests. As a Canadian she knew there was more than one way of doing most things.

Their evening had included the bats, for which Austin is famous, flowing out at dusk from their roosts under the bridge, over the Lady Bird Lake and on to the far horizon.

The bridge in question was the one that I had got to know as

I traversed it with repeated buses, the bridge of Congress Avenue over the Lady Bird Lake. It had been rebuilt in 1980 in such a way that the crevices under the bridge were appealing to Mexican free-tailed bats. They flew up from Mexico to Austin in March and stayed for the summer, giving a display at dusk as they flew out to dinner (all 1.5 million of them). Mr and Mrs Calgary recommended going to see the bats. Knowing that the bats flew at dusk because that was when their tasty meals of insects were ready to be eaten, I was not sure I wanted to expose myself to those self-same insects, providing them with the chance to make a meal of me.

~

I was down to my last pair of socks so my mission on my second Monday evening was the laundrette, not a place that proper Travellers would concern themselves with, but a reality I needed to face on a five-week trip. Early evening on a Monday should mean there would be plenty of unoccupied washers and driers, unlike at the peak of the weekend.

In preparation I had been saving a weight of quarters assiduously: nine for the washing machine and I hoped three would be enough for the drier. B&B host Eric gave me a cup of washing liquid. I made my way to the street corner laundrette, clasping my dirty washing to me. My natural preference is to fill up my car with fuel when the tank is only two-thirds empty so, while I knew a part-washload at the laundrette would make no sense, going down to my last pair of socks was not my usual way. Taking all the clothes I had and submitting them to machinery whose foibles I did not know, made me feel, well I suppose the right word is vulnerable.

I fed the Speed Queen my clothes, Eric's washing liquid and the quarters she required. She told me I had 34 minutes to watch others folding their laundry. One of the folders of laundry was beyond his last pair of socks, wearing one short black ankle sock and a longer, mid-calf, beige, ribbed sock. Various event posters flapped under the breeze from the laundrette's circling fans. The laundrette was clean and orderly, well-used by older college students.

Outside the laundrette, two very glossy black birds were enjoying a small puddle of water, flapping like excited toddlers, their tails fanning out, shading into blue as they turned towards the evening sunlight. I can enjoy flowers for just being pink or yellow, but not knowing a bird's name reminded me I was in a foreign land. That was not necessarily a bad thing or a sad thing. It was just a reminder of a fact.

The Speed Queen's minutes ticked down. Three of us were waiting for our washers to finish spinning when a drunk brought his fug of cigarette smoke through the laundrette, disturbing the almost library-like calm. Like the other two I shook my head in answer to the unasked question and he left us to find someone he could beg some money from.

I celebrated my completed laundry at the local grill with a beer and the Dish of the Day, southern fried chicken, of which the best part was the sidekick of broccoli. Nothing had been done to that. The chicken itself was fine, once I got to it, digging through the fried layers of stuff that might once have been bread crumbs and were what made it an authentic experience I am sure, but not one I would search out to repeat.

4

April on the road without MacNeice

All of a sudden I had read all 21 boxes of manuscripts in the MacNeice collection in the University of Texas' Humanities Research Center. I had spent my ten days in library calm and had had more than two long weekends-worth of enjoying the sights and sounds of being a tourist in Austin. It was time to pack up, to leave the human-scale domesticity of 'my' Austin neighbourhood of Hyde Park and head off to what that fallible oracle of the internet told me was the 49th (out of a poll of 50) most walkable of the larger US cities.

My next stop was Charlotte, North Carolina, which had absolutely no MacNeice connection. I had decided to stop in Charlotte long enough to have a look around just because this was the airport where I needed to change planes to get to Wilmington and Wilmington was where I needed to be to board my containership home.

Charlotte's downtown was referred to as uptown and that was where I stayed for two days, away from laundrettes and neighbourhood restaurants, back in the land of business suits and briefcases, a place of glass-fronted skyscrapers, smeared, when I arrived, in a drizzly mist.

I sat quietly in my hotel room with a map from the hotel's front desk, my ears still ringing with the amount of personal information shared by my seat neighbour on the flight over from Austin. She had been a nurse before setting up a business with her husband and was only based in Austin in cooler months, living her summers on an island in Minnesota that her dad bought after the war, though her mom was no longer able to make the journey, which was why she and her doctor sister were on the flight to visit her. In her slight pause for breath I wondered how much of my peculiar truth to reveal. I settled for saying that I was spending a couple of days in Charlotte before going home to the UK and I had spent some time being a tourist in Austin. All of which was true and sufficiently edited to sound plausible.

The phrase 'missing you already' drifted through my mind from Austin, but I told myself that I would, with luck and a little application, find an interesting two days of things to do and see in Charlotte, despite the forecast of steady rain.

~

The forecast was not wrong. After two days of rain (some of it heavy and all of it wet), I was packed up again, waiting at the bus stop for the airport shuttle bus to Charlotte Douglas International Airport and my short hop onwards to Wilmington, North Carolina. On the more positive side, with luck and a little application I had indeed found an interesting two days of things to do and see in Charlotte.

That first evening I happened upon an eating place, with beer being visibly brewed in the passageway behind the restaurant which served sturdy and straightforward meals.

Before the rain really set in the next morning I had discovered that there was an open weekend of ten gardens in the historic Fourth District area of Charlotte. Being late April their hellebores were still going strong, but their roses were also in bloom; one had such a scent that even I could smell it, hanging over the pathway, suffusing the air with the promise of summer. There were fiercely clipped, ankle-high box hedges throughout and plenty of hostas in their shady places, lacking the slugholes of hostas in south London. One gardener had mulched his larger planted pots with old wine corks. Another had a big terracotta pot, planted full of coiled hosepipe. A third described the steady noise of the main road behind her trees as an urban ocean. Listening to the waves of sound, rising and falling in the background, I could understand its similarly lulling effect.

Outside the front door nearly all the houses had wicker chairs or wooden swing benches, dreaming of soft evenings of recollection. Leaving furniture outside the front of the house is not something I do in south London. We do not have the weather for it and, in my case, I would be thoroughly nibbled by biting insects if I sat around, exposing flesh, at dusk.

I passed a manhole cover. It declared, in blue spray paint, 'Do not pick up.' I caught myself wondering what would happen if I did pick it up, what might lurk underneath: installation art or municipal stench?

Once the rain in a place has really set in, my usual riposte is to find a museum and Charlotte obliged with the Levine Museum of the New South, an absorbing and well-laid out two hours focused on the south and on history from the time of the civil war onwards. Towards the end of their displays was a set of sliding buttons to gauge whether your manner of speech was more from the north (direct and task-orientated) or from the south (indirect and putting relationships first). My choice of button positions put me firmly from the north.

When I came to buy a ticket to the Charlotte Symphony, I had to rein myself in while waiting for the customer in front to draw their discursive conversation to a close and then, only partially-trained in such things, I too had a conversational canticle of verse and response across a range of topics, while buying my concert ticket.

The concert started with two Dutch brothers (Lucas and Arthur Jussen) performing Mozart's Concerto for two pianos, followed by a touching presentation to the retiring bass trombone with the orchestra for 38 years and then we were swept through Mendelssohn's cheerful *Italian Symphony*. Less good was the amount of talking during the concert. Perhaps the audience was deafer than I am used to in London and so assumed others could not hear what they thought were imperceptible whisperings? Or perhaps they were all so in tune with their normality of keeping a continuous commentary flowing through their online social networks that they carried that behaviour everywhere, even into the concert hall?

The following evening I happened upon an end of year performance by The Carolinas Latin Dance Company, a youth dance organisation based in Charlotte (dancers aged about 5 to early 20s) doing a series of traditional dances from all over Latin America. The audience of parents and extended family seemed very Hispanic, all very voluble and with little English being spoken. Many held bunches of flowers, which I discovered were to present to 'their' dancer at the end of the evening. Considerable work (no doubt for the mothers) had gone into all the costumes, as the dancers for each dance wore something appropriate to the country of the dance's origin, including some very frilly, and aerodynamically suited for flouncing, flamenco skirts for the intermediate girls,

Each dance had a scripted introduction in Spanish by a man and then its translation in English by a lady. They added to the variety of the evening with frequent dress changes, some more flattering than others. This meant that at one point, although the lady was fully re-dressed when she came back on stage, she had to admit (to much sympathetic laughter) that she had left her glasses behind somewhere.

There was a dance from Mexico that involved tap dancing on a small wooden box, balancing a glass of water on the dancer's head. The boy in the group had a wet shirt clinging to his back by the time the music stopped. There was a dance from Honduras that involved (as several later dances did too) much hip wriggling – an eight-year old girl in glasses led that with some style. The older students had graduated to dances with shoulder-shaking that was independently articulated from their hip-wriggling. A Bolivian dance required three teenage boys to wear boots with bells on. One boy was concentrating very hard and looking very serious; one was slightly less serious of face and had still got most of the moves; while the third was really enjoying himself, but some of his moves verged on the impromptu.

My seat neighbours in the theatre had Peruvian heritage and became even more animated when it was the turn of a Peruvian dance on the programme. They obviously really wanted something to rival the Columbian and Puerto Rican foot-stompers we had had earlier in the evening – and so did I for their sakes – but sadly the Peruvian dance was a quieter and less involving one.

One dance had a call from the dancers to which the entire audience (other than me, the small Brit sitting in a Peruvian row) knew the response to sing back to the dancers. There was a guest troupe from Brazil, doing a type of martial arts dance (Capoeira) that included a beefy bloke, almost as wide as he was tall, throwing himself head first into a hands-free cartwheel across the stage.

For me the best dance was a Colombian one, choreographed to involve the whole company, smuggling the smallest dancers on while you were watching the middle-sized ones and then the oldest students appearing, while you were smiling at the smallest boy being shepherded through his moves by two girls of his own size, but who had been paying more attention in rehearsals.

A thoroughly 'feel good' evening – and the rain had stopped for my short walk home to the hotel after the show.

~

The next instalment of this chapter was waiting in Wilmington. I had scheduled a handful of days in Wilmington to allow for any changes in the timetable of the ship I had booked on and any attendant bureaucracy, arising from doing something barely on the fringes of normal.

I had another hotel room to occupy and another map of the downtown area to plan with. This room had a sweeping view of Cape Fear River, with moored working vessels attached to jetties and over on the far side the imposing bulk of USS *North Carolina* that had been a tourist attraction since she arrived there in the 1960s.

Leaving Charlotte had not improved the weather forecast. I needed to find some more museums, though, as a fallback, the desk in my Wilmington hotel room was large and had a good light and I consoled myself with the thought that I did not have to wait until I got on board ship to start typing up my notes from Austin's reading room.

I started the morning with a call to the port agent. We established that I was not the Man from California that the agent was expecting to call. I sent an email to my contact in London to wrinkle out whether Woman from south London had somehow been conflated with Man from California and then, with rain imminent, I set off to my first museum, just outside the door of my hotel, the Wilmington Railroad Museum.

The enthusiastic volunteer on the front desk taking entrance fees agreed that the weather was unseasonably cold and started in on telling me more than I might need to know about the history of the museum. Fortuitously I was relieved of listening duties by the entrance of two holidaying families and their energetic small children.

The display cabinet told me that by 1840 the Wilmington and

Raleigh Rail Road had 161 miles of track. Given it was only in 1829 that Stephenson's *Rocket* won the Rainhill Trials and the prize of running on the Liverpool and Manchester Railway Company, that did seem a swiftly comprehensive adoption of new technology. The report of the opening of the Rail Road had the glorious phrase, 'Good cheer gave quick wings to nurslings of wit'.

While I could understand how the south was hampered during the civil war by having six different gauges of railway lines, I could not get my head round the label that declared that in 12 hours in 1886 the whole of the US changed to one gauge.

An employment application from 1949 asked, 'Are you financially involved?' and I wondered what that meant.

I smiled at the description of the railroad president (travelling around his railroad network in his own adapted railroad car) being accompanied by an 'all purpose steward and travelling secretary'. I had an inkling of what that meant.

The museum's labels offered a whole new line of enquiry for the mildly curious. How about the backstory to Elijah McCoy (1843–1929) a mechanic and engineer who had 57 patents to his name by his death and was said to be the source of the phrase 'the real McCoy'? He was the son of slaves who ran away to Canada and he himself went to Scotland to do his training. Was the weather for him in Scotland better than he was used to in Canada?

The back room in the museum had an intricate model railway layout, with green buttons to push to set sections of it off and running through its precisely modelled world. There was a list of the features of a good model railroad layout – one of which, somewhat startlingly, was 'bulletproof trackwork'. Certainly this layout had impressive attention to detail and careful choice of the detail to attend to. The most unusual feature was a tiny video camera, mounted on one of the trains, that was linked to a TV screen in the corner of the room, showing the view from the train. I saw the arm of my jacket on that screen as the train went by so I knew it was not rerunning an old recording.

At the back of the main display was a town square on a smaller scale. The label told me that this N-scale layout was donated by a former member of the modelling club when, aged 90, he moved to Arizona. That conjured up some backstory. I suspected there was also at least mild concern about mixing two scales in one layout.

I left my speculation and went back outside where the rain had stopped, but there was no sunlight yet.

I continued my time of being a tourist, with a meal of shrimps wrapped in bacon, dunked in barbecue sauce, in a tented and decked area at one of several restaurants lining the river. Some customers were more confident, sitting out in the open; others opted for the full protection of sitting inside. Under canvas I started to worry about biting insects. It was time to move briskly on.

Despite the fact I was about to be on board a ship for at least ten days, I went in search of the tourist boats that ran trips up and down the river. I weighed up the options. There might be a larger vessel going out for 90 minutes later in the afternoon, but only if there were at least 15 passengers. Given the number of people I had not seen as I walked from the museum to the riverfront that seemed unlikely on such an unprepossessing day. The alternative was a small boat going in a few minutes, with just one passenger, me, on it.

The small boat was called *Capt Maffitt* and her two crew and I spent a windswept hour heading up and down river. We got a good view of the brown pelicans, skimming low and then coming in to land on the river, feet first. They looked as built by committee as their white brethren, but being brown the overall impression was more mundane and not as exotic as the more picturebook white pelicans.

I heard the stories of USS *North Carolina*, the nickel and dime collections to save her from the scrapyard and bring her home. Some excited terns darted about us, until they got bored and flitted off.

There was the story of the rice planting on Eagles Island. A cautionary tale if ever there was one. The rice harvest on Eagles Island was good, in fact so good that the owners wanted to bring in bigger boats to make it easier to take the harvest away to the markets. To do that they needed to dredge the river. In dredging they changed the flow of water in the main river channel. That meant more sea water came further up the river. The salt water made the river water brackish. The fields irrigated with brackish water yielded no more rice harvests.

We chugged towards the port of Wilmington. As we passed alongside another containership, the idea of getting on such a ship and going home that way seemed even more improbable. I could see a ship, with gangway, berthed where 'my' ship would be berthed in a day or two. I could see the reality of a rainbow of containers boxed across the decks. I could not see me, transposed from being a tourist bobbing about in a tourist boat, hearing snippets of history and geography and local tales of the river, to being a transatlantic passenger, cresting the ocean wave.

Back on dry land I eyed up a restaurant for my evening meal. After my brush with southern fried chicken in Austin I decided I should try again with 'southern' dishes. The starter had to be Fried Green Tomatoes, such an evocative name. The mustard on them had some kick and I liked their onions, but lathering fried stuff on something does not, for me, improve the underlying something.

I was seated at a table looking out over the street so could not see my fellow diners, but once in a while a sentence hung in the air above the restaurant's tables.

'Did I know she was pregnant?' That came with a strong implication that the She in question should have told the speaker herself.

'I am not a sand person.' Frying noises from the kitchen prevented me from hearing what the alternative was to being a sand person.

A lady extolled the many virtues of a youngster, 'She's so active, so quick to learn, so loving' and then I realised she was describing a new puppy, not a baby granddaughter.

There was a level of background music and general chatter that meant it was only the loudest of speakers whose pronouncements rang across the room, but the music suddenly stopped so the whole room heard, not only the question, 'What was he like?' but also the answering admission, 'I had wine at lunch.'

I chose pulled pork as my main course and added a side order of another dish that I had to try while in that part of the world: Mac'n'cheese. My verdict? Plenty of mac and not a lot of cheese. Still I am in no position to judge whether those renditions were in fact just as they should be. I have no benchmark to compare them with.

Given American portion sizes I had in Texas often been eating a starter as my main course, but talking to the waiter I discovered that the restaurant offered smaller portions so customers could have all three courses (and the restaurant had the sense to put a smaller price on the smaller portion option). Result.

Even more of a result was the dessert. I have no idea whether that too was a southern speciality or indeed what it should have tasted like, but for me their Coca-cola cake was a triumph.

I negotiated the bill/check/notes linguistic divide and left. Outside there was the possibility of a sunset, or more particularly a sunset that could be photographed. The clouds (and you do need a few to make a good sunset picture) had some breaks in them. I considered the options for my foreground. There was a row of wooden benches that looked promising, but when I got down to their level I was greeted by an immovable rubbish bin. Maybe not. Further on were some poles. They were tall and their reflections were commensurately deep, but the clouds, after their trial separation were getting back together. It was not going to be the night for a photogenic sunset after all.

Or maybe?

Just before I reached my hotel I paused to wonder about the possibilities offered by the ladders of light, spotlighting some rusty machinery on the far bank of the river, but even as I had the thought the ladders were pulled up.

I am the child of my father who had a hobby of taking (and developing at home) black and white photographs – landscapes for preference – and I spent a portion of my childhood on expeditions with him, waiting for the light to change.

It always did, but not necessarily for the better.

He it was who showed me bending your knees or leaning in or out when taking photographs, looking for a different view, not forgetting the view behind you. Then there were the thirds. Not to divide the frame into two halves, but to look for the more satisfying thirds. In the ideal world you would then locate an obedient seagull or sheep (depending on your terrain) to stand at the intersection of the bottom left thirds, but that, like pink-fingered sunsets, was not often achieved.

Waiting for unphotogenic sunsets was a childhood memory of summer holidays, once I was old enough to be up that late. I knew from a young age the falsity of the tagline that the camera never lies. I had been allowed into my father's darkroom. I had seen things not appear in the developing tray.

Squabbling seagulls arguing over whose fish it really was brought me back to 2013. Just beyond them a sleek and solitary diver, a cormorant perhaps, was going about his fishing, without drawing any attention to himself. An arrowhead of ducks flew home to roost, looking just like those much derided ornaments in the front rooms of houses of a certain age.

It started to rain again. A pair of walkers, with severely vigorous, arm-pumping action, strode, as one, past me.

Another morning. Another call to the port agent. He had heard from the vessel's captain. I was on the captain's list as an onward passenger from Wilmington.

My next call was to US Customs and Border Protection in Wilmington to check whether it was the port agent, the captain or me who needed to register with them the fact of my leaving the US, to which the answer was that the captain put in the paperwork to them. They did not need to see either me or my passport. I sent an updating email to London and then set off under cloudy skies for another museum.

En route I 'blew in' to browse a book shop. The owner said most of her customers blew in, not because they wanted to buy a book but because they were browsing the shops in the area. That meant gifts and cards made up a significant proportion of her sales and of the books she did sell around a third were 'beach fiction'. One of the books I bought was about Emily Dickinson's correspondence with one Thomas Wentworth Higginson. It was not in the style I intended to be writing in, so it too was escapism in its way, though not what you might think of as beach reading. Indeed of all the places on my list of possible itineraries, none was a beach for reading on. The other book I bought was nearer to what I am writing – it had a road trip from New Jersey to Chicago as the backdrop to its main plot.

~

As well as being a tourist boat yesterday, I learnt Captain Maffitt was one of those who ran the Union blockade of Wilmington at the time of the civil war. The Cape Fear Museum was another museum that focused its energy from the time of the American civil war onwards and for me the museum drew out how the choices at that time in that part of the world might have seemed less clear-cut than they did subsequently to the victors in the north, who wrote the history.

One of the temporary exhibitions in the Cape Fear Museum took a series of objects from that period and set out what was known about that object, what might be inferred from its circumstances and what questions were begged between the known facts and the inferred context. That room also included a Confederacy flag, with its story attached of how one design had been turned down for not being sufficiently different from the Union flag and another had too much white on it so it was turned down for looking like a flag of surrender and for not being able to be seen clearly enough across water.

I got thoroughly confused about what the Democrats supported and what the Republicans supported from time to time in that era, but then I am no better on the Whigs and Tories of my own country's 19th century.

I enjoyed the evidence from the 1860 census of Wilmington being a well-balanced port with 13 ministers of religion and 13 bar-keepers.

Another temporary display in the Cape Fear Museum was from Cape Fear Camera Club: landscapes taken within ten miles of Wilmington. While they were not uniform in style, they were uniformly excellent. No duds had been left in the pack to encourage improvers.

~

The sun was thinking about coming out as I left the Cape Fear Museum. I arrived at the Bellamy Manson House between the tour times, so the volunteers gave me a set of headphones and an MP3 player to follow my own tour round the house built in 1860, just before the civil war broke out. The narrator started me in the five-seater privy and later took me up to that wonder of its time, the room built especially to hold a bath. My own house in deepest south London got one of those nearly 100 years later so I was suitably impressed.

The narrator warned me about the steepness of the back stairs. They were not as steep as my stairs at home, but curved in a more elegant way. I spent some happy moments trying to frame them in my camera, bending to and fro, leaning in and out. Not something I could have done if I had arrived at the proper time for a live tour.

The narrator in my ears had been given a script with a lightness of touch, some history and some excerpts read from letters of the time. The script took the listener through some of the house's architectural features, particularly those that would have helped to keep the house cooler in the summer months. Not something that was needed as I went round, but I could appreciate the dining room benefiting from being in the basement, only partly underground, like being in a brick-lined moat; though I wondered what had happened for such basements to be called 'English' basements? The observatory on the top of the house had windows that, when opened, would pull the hot air out. The sash windows for the main reception rooms went down to the floor so you could step, even in a long dress, over the sill and out on to the porch.

'Porch' to British ears might well be a lean-to, a transient place by an entrance door, a place of leaking waterproofs, tired sports equipment, muddy shoes and nearly-discarded umbrellas, whereas here porches were magnificent verandahs, with cushioned rocking chairs.

As I did in Austin and in Charlotte, I daydreamed a little about the parallel universe where I might have a wooden swing seat strapped to my rafters and the weather on insect-free evenings to enjoy such a seat. I suspected some of that dreaming was an echo from time spent with my New Zealand cousins on the wide verandah of their bungalow, looking out over their Waikato farm, enjoying the view from the friendly chairs that did not match each other, but welcomed whoever was passing their driveway.

It seems extraordinary in this internet age that aged 18 I wrote airmail letters (made of blue, tissue-thin paper, that you folded up and licked shut) and then got on a plane in London, which in those days was a foreign enough place, to meet the recipients of those letters. Once in New Zealand my (borrowed) brown suitcase and I got on buses to go from recipient to recipient. It was in the 1980s, before wheels (at least for luggage) had been invented and the case had two metal clasps, not a zipped circumference.

Back in 2013, I wended my way down to the riverfront via a series of knight's moves, along and across, showing me the historic district of Wilmington, clustered around Third Street, where the houses got left behind as the business of the 20th century moved inland. Having listened to the Bellamy Mansion House narrator I was now 'seeing' more of the features of the houses I passed, sunglasses on my nose, but still glad of my jacket.

This time on the riverfront I opted for high tea, thinking I would have some time to write up my impressions of Wilmington.

I did indeed have a high tea of seafood bisque, sandwiches, scones and cakes, all daintily presented and washed down with the tea of my choice, but I got far too distracted by my fellow customers to write up my impressions. They were a party of ladies getting together once a month, taking it in turns to choose the venue. Whether all the ladies could make the appointed first Wednesday did depend on such things as their grandchildren's sports matches and knee or hip replacements for them or their husbands or neighbours. The restaurant's service was at a leisurely pace, but then neither I nor the other ladies were having a business lunch or taking a break from our day's office work.

One of the ladies had been overseas once. She had been to Quebec, which was a mistake she was not going to repeat. That led on to several stories about what Europeans did on airplanes, for which I did not hear the punchlines, as I had to pay some attention to my own table to make some menu choices and understand the tea pot, which was set on a stand, warmed by a small candle, and guarded by an off-duty egg-timer with three separate phials, each a different colour and thickness of sand so I could choose the length of time I left the tea leaves to brew.

In talking about a possible future venue for the lunching ladies, one was crossed off as only a place for husbands to go. Another came with a description of how it was now where something else had been after that had moved from where it was, which used to be just across the street from another place some of them used to go to a lot when the children were small. I was not sure that either the speaker or her listeners had kept track of which was the restaurant being suggested for the next meal. One here or one in the previous century? The most organising of the ladies said she would send round an email about next month.

All in all Wilmington was a pleasant way to pass time. I enjoyed Wilmington (like Austin and indeed Charlotte) for being a place that did not bring with it a raft of touristic obligations, things that must be seen. No Big Ben or Eiffel Tower. Perhaps I enjoyed it all the more, because it was so unexpected. I had quite thought Wilmington would be some early typing in my hotel room at the broad and well-lit desk, which was what I did end up doing on my last afternoon there as the rain came down much more heavily.

~

Next morning I made a phone call to the taxi firm that had all the accreditations to be able to drive me to the port of Wilmington, through its gates, across the operating areas and then drop me at the vessel's berth. I booked the taxi for noon, as suggested by the port agent, so I could board when the longshoremen were on their lunch break and the port's loading operations were paused.

Time to pack again. Time to leave again a place that I had become accustomed to.

The CCTV camera in the hotel grounds below my window was mounted on a pole that also had a nest box attached to it, which had been taken on by a pair of busy sparrows. I watched them for a while and then the seagulls wheeling over the Cape Fear River. The wind ruffled the river at an angle to the tide's direction.

Then I turned back to my list of things To Do. Some were to do while I still had an internet connection: fully answering my email inbox and doing some research on the onward travel options from Antwerp in two weeks' time. For that I had to fight the algorithms that insisted I must really, deep down, be interested in a return trip to Antwerp that started in London, and not the single leg from Antwerp to London that I typed in.

Just because I could, I wondered off at an internet tangent looking for the Elijah McCoy whom I met in the Wilmington Railroad Museum. As well as the more serious business of moving lubrication smoothly forward with his numerous lubricant patents, Elijah appeared to have also invented, or certainly improved, a portable ironing table and a lawn sprinkler.

~

I checked out of my room, watching the falling rain as I sat in the hotel's reception area, listening to the phone calls ringing to cancel bookings made for the coming weekend.

I waited.

Just at the point when I thought that perhaps I should ring to see that my booking was recorded, a taxi pulled up.

'Are you only one?'

'Yes Sir.' I had been in town long enough to add a Sir or Ma'am when answering pointed questions.

Having spent some time earlier in the week disentangling my identity from that of the Man from California, I did wonder whether this was 'my' taxi. Had the driver been sent to collect a more orthodox couple?

We established that he was expecting to take however many passengers there were from this hotel to 'my' containership and that he had the paperwork to fill in to get me through the port gates, so we set off to my next instalment.

It was still raining.

5

May at sea

I left my known world of land-based activity and entered through the gates of the Port of Wilmington. Here, even on land, the activity was directed out to sea, to a world I knew enough about to know how little of it I knew.

The taxi stopped on the landward side of the deeply-inset rails that the port's cranes inch along when they are working. They were not working. It was lunchtime and they were still.

I paid my taxi fare. It was still raining, steadily, not torrentially. My wheeled, blue suitcase looked effete in such a setting. I grasped its handle firmly and set off, at what I hoped was sufficient speed to get across the crane rails without one of the suitcase wheels getting caught in one of the gaps between rail and concrete. At least it was obvious that I was in the right place. Unlike the B&B in Austin, the ship had a clearly painted name.

It was raining too much for a pose at the stern of the berthed ship. Not that there was anyone about to take such a photograph, one of me embarking on one of those ideas that seemed a good one at the time.

I trundled along the concrete at the side of the ship to the gangway, feeling mildly put out that North Carolina was raining on me as if I were at home in south London.

At the foot of the gangway I peered out from under the hood of my waterproof and saw the cheerful sight of a boiler-suited Filipino seaman coming down the gangway towards me. We agreed (checking our watches) that it was time to say good afternoon so we said, 'Good afternoon.' He swung my suitcase ahead of him and at the top of the gangway I signed in. A brief walkie-talkie exchange ensued about where to put me. I was put in the deck office.

The cook greeted me and made sure I knew that the next meal would not be served in the officers' mess until 1730 hours. He was very keen to make sure that I understood where the officers' mess was and that I would be able to last the next five hours. I assured him I had some food and drink with me. (I had read the small print in the pre-boarding information.)

The second officer greeted me, locked my passport in the safe ('until Antwerp') and gave me directions to the fourth deck where I would, he said, find my cabin.

Out to the corridor I went, but I failed to locate the stairs up to the fourth deck.

I went back to the deck office, by which time a US official was quizzing the second officer about the requisite inspection of 'trash arrangements'. I felt awkward asking about the missing stairs. Another crew member took me to the right door and (a key feature) unlocked it. I did then manage to go up the necessary flights of stairs to the fourth deck. I heaved on the firmly-sprung door from the staircase to the corridor of the fourth deck. I continued to the far end of the corridor, only to find that the door to the Supercargo cabin, my home for the next ten days, was locked.

Back down I went to the deck office, feeling even more sharply the awkwardness of my inability to follow simple directions.

The trash arrangements had been dealt with and the second officer came with me back up to the fourth deck, unlocked my door, and in his best Germanic English suggested that I now rest in my cabin. I took that to be an entirely fair suggestion that I keep out of the way for the remainder of the afternoon.

I surveyed my suite, for it was more than just the sleeping space and limited storage space that the word 'cabin' conveyed to me. It had a shower, basin and toilet as an ensuite to a room with a bed and a wardrobe, which itself opened onto my main room, furnished with a sofa, a bench, a table, a soft chair, another wardrobe, another chair and then the crowning glory of a desk that was larger than the desk I have at home.

I looked out of each of my three portholes, one in the bedroom and one in the main room, both looking over the stern where the German flag flew and a second porthole in the main room, next to my desk, with a rainswept view of the port operations resuming after lunch. I re-examined each porthole in turn, but none of them were suitable for opening. Even with my sense of smell I had already noticed that the previous occupant of the Supercargo cabin was a smoker, a heavy smoker. I began to wonder what food would be served at 1730. Would it be a pungent dish? Perhaps I could borrow a bowl of strong curry to mask the smell of fetid tobacco? The most strongly-smelling item in my luggage was a box of lemon and ginger teabags that I had bought in Wilmington as supplementary supplies. Somehow it seemed unlikely that even a well-ordered German-flagged ship would have air freshener in its stores, but it might yet be a question to ask.

A Filipino seaman materialised at my door with a suitcase, which I tried to explain was not mine. Mine was the blue suitcase just inside the door of the deck office. I suspected that the proffered brown case belonged to the Man from California, but decided not to confuse matters by speculating aloud to someone whose first language was not English. A few moments later the seaman reappeared with my suitcase.

I unpacked and explored my new quarters. There were two large canvases of framed artwork in my main room. One was a succession of differently-coloured inkblots, fading into each other. The other was a sweep of thick brushstrokes, each clotted with a single colour. Not what I would have at home, not least because I do not have that amount of flat and empty wall.

There was a fridge under my desk (something else I do not have at home) with several cans of fizzy drinks (the full-fat versions) and a bottle of German beer. Inside one of the desk drawers was a bottle opener and a long rectangle of white matting, the sort that had a stickiness about it to stop things from sliding around. I placed the matting on my desk in expectation of having weather that would deserve it. I put my alarm clock and torch by my bed, but cushioned in a towel, in the hope that would stop them moving once we got under way. Bed, desk, sofa, bench, fridge and both wardrobes were securely affixed to the floor. There was a rubbish bin that, like the chairs, was unattached. I spent some time wondering whether there was a way of attaching the bin to the sofa with the piece of elasticated rope with two rubber-coated metal hooks that was loose on the sofa. It was the sort of 'spider leg' that in the summer holidays of my childhood we used to strap luggage to the car's roof-rack before we set off to north Cornwall.

Another person materialised at my door: weather-burnt face, framed by a mane of free-flowing white hair, punctuated with two gold ear-rings. He would not have looked out of place in one of the country music bands in Austin. The ship's captain introduced himself in lightly-accented English. He explained how the elasticated rope hooked the main cabin door safely open, by attaching the other hook to the wardrobe door in my main room. He mentioned how things would move around once we left the Cape Fear River. There would be, maybe a day, or perhaps a day and a half, of the ship moving around he said. He illustrated the possibility with an indeterminate motion of his hand. He cautioned against going out on deck while there was this moving around. I assured him I would not go outside. I would hold onto the handrail in the corridor. I would make sure I applied three points of contact on the stairways when I was moving around when the ship was doing her moving around.

I left my cabin door hooked open, in the hope of some corridor air diluting my cabin air before the start of the promised moving around.

They had docked in Wilmington at 0600 hours and planned on leaving soon after 1700 hours, long enough for one set of containers to be unloaded and another set loaded and time for those who were up all night working with the pilot, guiding the ship up the Cape Fear River, to have some sleep, before the process was reversed.

From my porthole vantage point, two decks below the bridge, I watched the containers being moved by fork-lift vehicles. These were no ordinary fork-lifts. They were on steroids. Each fork-lift had a long width of pincer by which it grasped a single container. The fork-lift took each container, a building block from a stack four-high on the concrete, and positioned it on a wheeled bed pulled by a white cab. Each white cab was driven off in a certain order, directed by a hard hat and fluorescent jacket, a lone figure on the concrete. A succession of white cabs lined up for the crane on rails to grasp in its turn each chosen container and lift it onto the ever-growing pile of building blocks on our deck.

To my surprise nearly all the containers we were gathering were a deep red, not the rainbow of different colours, the assortment of house colours of owners and lessees that I was expecting to see. The ship's three yellow, deck-mounted cranes were idle. The blue legs of the Port of Wilmington's crane were doing all the work, beeping insistently as they moved slightly to and fro on the deeply-inset rails to adjust the alignment of each box the crane lowered.

Enjoyable though it was to watch others work, I powered up my laptop and began to put finger to keyboard in my own task of building, first spreading my notes from Austin across my desk, then clustering them into themes. I was relieved that the continental adaptor plug worked. I was even more relieved when I noticed that the air-conditioning had cranked into life, an ally against my cabin's tobacco smell.

Typing my way into my notes also put my embarkation nerves down where they belonged, below the items labelled 'not a priority'. Setting off by containership to Antwerp in some ways was no different from leaving my south London front door for a west London dinner party, something I do not look forward to, but I can tell myself I will be fine when under way. Though this time I did admit there were some differences. There was not even the theoretical possibility of bailing out before coffee.

Suddenly it was 1730 hours. I made my way down to the first deck. I tested my strength against another highly-sprung door and located dinner. It was pasta with beef stew, tasty enough, but not nearly strong-smelling enough to overcome the tobacco smell if the air-conditioning did not master it by nightfall.

Everyone was working as we prepared to leave port so dinner was just me and the Man from California, a retired lawyer.

I too admitted to being a lawyer, one from London, who began my professional life in ship financing. Since then, I said, curiosity had led me to holiday on a tall ship sailing in and out of some of the islands of Vanuatu in the South Pacific and on the flagship of Trinity House, watching her crew repair and maintain lightships and buoys in English waters. I also admitted to having crossed the Equator at sea, on a voyage by mail ship back to the UK from St Helena.

I decided that was more than enough shipping information and left out the perversity of going by sea to the Faroe Islands for a holiday and any mention of two of my more memorable business trips, going to Poland for a ship's christening and crossing the English Channel on the bridge of a ferry.

The Man from California, although he started the voyage by flying across three time zones from California to Wilmington, had decided travelling by sea was a good way to avoid jetlag. He had not convinced his wife, who was flying over to meet him in Amsterdam for their month of holiday in Europe.

I did also admit to travelling by sea because I thought it would be a place with no distractions from my typing a draft book. (I left Louis MacNeice's name out of it, for the time being at least.)

The tone of the engine changed. We both rapidly finished our plates and went to watch Wilmington recede.

For once it was an archetypal summer evening. No biting insects about. A stray swallow looped past me. The pilot was on the bridge in chinos and a checked shirt, making arrangements with two, deep-red tug-boats guiding a Liberian-flagged Chinese-named vessel into the berth we had just left.

I found a sunny spot on deck, nearly sheltered from the wind, and watched the river unwind between red and green buoys under streaky wisps of cloud. The feeling of Just Being warmed me and behind that were unfocused memories of all the best parts of the many ferry journeys I had taken over the years.

A whole class of over-excited gulls were chasing our wake to see if we might turn up anything of interest. They reminded me of the farm dogs on my cousins' farm in New Zealand that chased cars down the drive, more for sport than in earnest.

A couple of more measured pelicans flew to one side of the gulls, just in case our wake did turn something up. We passed a series of randomly scattered small islands that illustrated, as the Cape Fear Museum had said, the difficulties of blockading Wilmington at the time of the civil war. I wondered whether the houses with their long piers were lived in year-round or bought with an unrealised intention of long storybook holidays.

As we reached the mouth of the river more angular terns joined us and some gannets swooped alongside, both birds I associated with coastal waters. In view of the captain's forecast, it was time to go below.

~

From the vantage point of typing this up, I can admit that for the first morning at sea I was not my best self or even my second or third best self. My body did not approve of this idea of coming home on a containership. That was in part because of a very disjointed night of interrupted sleep, waking up every other pitch and roll, shaken by the engine vibrations and questioning each new noise, each change in tone of the engine and of the wind. I somewhat queasily made it back from that first morning's breakfast, struggling a little more with each of the succession of highly-sprung doors.

My body was not impressed and I could see her point. There was a regular, and relatively steady, rolling of the ship into which, at irregular intervals, was thrown a pitch forward that was then yanked backwards, like a dog on one of those adjustable leads, suddenly being jerked back after running the lead out beyond where it should. From my desk I could see two portholes and, from time to time, two horizons so I camped there, concentrating on the horizons, in between dozing with my head on the desk cushioned by my fleece jacket.

Having forced my body to breakfast at 0730 hours she did a deal with me and we missed lunch at 1145 hours.

All of a sudden it was early afternoon. I woke up, hungry, and snacked on some of the supplementary supplies I had bought in Wilmington, a box of what I called biscuits but which the shopkeeper had only been able to find for me when we had worked out that I was looking for what he called crackers.

Both portholes still had views that went, at not very regular intervals, from being one-third water to all sky and then back again to being one-third water. Nothing had changed outside, but I was suddenly back in one piece. I had been given some sea legs and my body and I were reattached into one functioning whole, equilibrium restored.

I applied myself to putting on my rubber-gripped shoes and tacking my way down the corridor and up, by the internal stairs, to the bridge, where the officer of the watch was just percolating a jug of coffee to a soundtrack of throbbing heavy metal, that deserved an outbreak of air-drumming, not just air guitars. The windscreen wipers were clearing his chosen set of windows so we had a proper view of the sea's swell. He estimated we were being hit by 25-plus knots of wind and four metre swells. I accepted a half-full mug of coffee (anything more would have been unwise given my inexperience in the sea conditions).

It no longer seemed a bad idea, coming home by containership.

As far as the Beaufort scale was concerned we had got perhaps up to force 7.

Beaufort was a senior administrator in the 19th century

British navy who standardised the descriptions used for weather observations on the high seas into a 12 point scale. Although I did not grow up by the sea and have no history of time spent in yachts or dinghies, I knew from my childhood about Beaufort, thanks to the BBC's *Shipping Forecast* (a report on the current weather of, and future forecast for, the sea areas around the British Isles, which precedes the main radio weather forecast and sounds evocative of a certain order, even if the forecast itself is disturbingly rough).

In the stiff upper lip terminology of the 19th century force 7 was only one notch up from a strong breeze. When I read the more detailed descriptions used now, force 7 did sound more impressive: on land it requires effort to walk and whole trees are in motion, while the sea is described as heaping up, with some foam from breaking waves blown into streaks along the wind direction and moderate amounts of airborne spray.

With a change of watch officer the soundtrack for the bridge was changed to softer, wordless, electronic music. The new watchkeeping officer said he did listen to what he called industrial music but only when he was exercising. He began to describe the types of martial arts he had moved on to when, after losing the fourth of his front teeth, he had decided his boxing days were over. He dismissed judo, because it depended on wearing a white jacket and was a recent invention, something made simple for foreigners. Karate was about speed in a small place, like bullets. Mixed martial arts was full contact, with gloves and some rules, but he found other amateurs were only brave with the punch bag.

The tattoos on his arms were revealed in technicolour, as he emphasised with his hands, his point about the benefits for a martial artist of being at sea, the benefits of developing the feeling in the gut, the knowledge in the body of where the centre of gravity is. He moved in one-sided illustration of using an opponent's kinetic energy, redirected, into your moves.

I knew from the pre-boarding information that there was both a gym and a swimming pool on board but had already decided not to frequent that part of the accommodation block. It belonged to the off-duty, relaxation time of the 21 male crew members. As the watch officer moved on to describe the benefits of his particular forms of exercise and what impact that had on the distribution of fat and muscle, and indeed how such distribution of fat and muscle should differ from the male to female form, I was happy with my decision. For the next ten days my exercise would be walking laps to the front end (or more technically to the bow) and back only if the sea was nearly flat. Otherwise my exercise would be heaving on the highly-sprung doors and stepping up and down the flights of stairs to meals and to such unexpectedly random conversations as I found on the bridge.

While I was thinking about not being in the gym the watch officer had moved on to the subject of alcohol. How can you drink responsibly? Is it responsible not to hit your friend when you drink? Is it responsible not to hit him if he has done something he should not do? That is what friends are for, to hit when they should. He tells me he does not drink alcohol at sea. Why would you? You have no friends who are personal, no nice place to go with your wife.

~

Two days in to our time at sea the captain felt it was safe enough for the two passengers to be allowed out on to the deck and therefore to have the full version of the safety briefing, complete with tour of the main points of interest: the location of the lifebelts to throw to someone who went overboard; the methods by which the various types of life boat and raft could be launched; muster points and water hydrants; secondary options and who could do what with the carbon dioxide bottles; life jackets and immersion suits (which looked on the large size for me and the Filipino officer performing the tour). It was all there, all emphasising just how far away we were from my known world of land-based activity. We made our way to the bow, the engine noise and associated vibrations fading as we advanced.

The ship was built in 2004, but was tidily kept, with a continual cycle of maintenance at sea, since there was no luxury of time for such things while on the tight turnarounds at the ports on this route. She was 207 metres long and had a beam of 29.8 metres. We were not quite fully loaded, so some twelve containers wide, three, four or, in parts, five containers tall and nine containers long. Unless the containers had declared dangerous cargo with submitted paperwork the crew did not know what was in the boxes, nor did anyone want to know, as they could not break the customs seal and do anything if the loads did start to move around. We had two containers of compressed gas. We had a couple of refrigerated containers and unsurprisingly their contents were described as foodstuffs.

The martial arts officer had mocked this route from the US to Europe and back as being like a computer game, just going from place to place, joining the dots, no thinking because no risk of capsizing the ship if the loading was wrong, but he too was glad of some time on a route without piracy and with straightforward port authorities. I heard stories of 'fines' for packets of lentils found in the storeroom that had no 'eat by' date on them and ports where you left anchorage and went 20-plus miles out to sea before dusk to be beyond the pirates, though if you came back to a new anchorage the next morning there would be another 'fine' for the same issue with the same packet of lentils, albeit at a different mooring.

By the third day on the open sea I did not need to think about the answer, I was enjoying myself, getting into a routine of writing between meals, interspersed with trips to the bridge to look at the weather forecast and have a more or less serious conversation, depending on the time of day, for, as well as different tastes in music, the watch officers had different tendencies in their topics of conversation.

The martial arts officer had a rapid-fire intensity. On another visit to the bridge of the ship I heard about his background reading for his small unit of social psychology studies and how what we think of ourselves, what others think of us and what we think others think of us can never be the same.

He told me he knew his studies on the effects of isolation would not change the world. Remembering how I got through what might have been boring times in my summer job in the caster wheel factory by categorising types of boredom, I could understand how studying the effects of isolation might help during four or more months at sea, with an occasional text message from the outside world whenever the ship is near enough to the shore to pick up a phone signal. Even for me, who enjoys my own company, I know there is an aching difference between the solitude you have chosen for a specific time or purpose and a gaping absence with no prospect of someone asking the questions you want to answer, no shared laughter from a common place.

The martial arts officer told me more about his small unit of social psychology studies, how, without language, we can not share memories. He and I can point to a table and see that is a table, whatever we call it, but we can not point to excitement and both know what that is.

~

The Man from California, with recently graduated children finding the US job market tough, was wondering, over one meal, about jobs at sea. Having heard him on the subject of jobs with a good healthcare package I wondered what he thought happened when a sailor got appendicitis and what about the short-term nature of each contract? Looking for a new job once or twice every year at sea sounded no better to me than the uncertainty his children were grappling with on land.

On land I have met people who live and breathe their work, but on board a containership there is no option. Everyone lives in their office. The four-hour rhythm of the watchkeepers drives through the days and the nights, the weeks and the weekends, indiscriminately. There can be no pushing on today to finish early tomorrow.

There is no warp and weft patterning of working relationships being built socially over time. If the officers or the crew socialise with anyone, it will be with their work colleagues, the people their lives depend on, who come and go at the crewing agency's direction.

I have read how some wicket-keepers in cricket matches switch off between each individual ball that is bowled so that they can keep their concentration for six hours behind the wicket. The noise of such a switching off from one day to the next reverberated down my corridor just before the evening meal. Now I had heard the term I think the reverberating noise could be described as 'industrial music'. It was computerised loops of vocals, fighting with bass drums, added to repetitive guitar chords that did not go anywhere.

The Man from California was one deck above me, sharing his corridor with the captain and chief engineer. The doors off my corridor led to the next level down in the officer hierarchy.

While the Man from California seemed somewhat surprised by the regularity with which the ship's time moved forward (six hours to be advanced in ten days did mean we only had a few nights without moving the clocks forward an hour) I had not realised just how much everything shook. Out in the bow, unseen by the bridge, it was quiet, but quietness in the accommodation block was a relative term, even outside the evening burst of industrial/relaxation music. What did not rattle, creaked or strained audibly.

My regular trips to the bridge helped me gauge the sea conditions and therefore when might be a better time to take a shower. We had a freshwater generator on board, boiling the seawater to leave the salt behind and cooling the steam back down, so we could be as profligate as we liked with drinking water and with showers, but combining water and shower gel with unannounced, sharply-lurching movements, required new skills.

From the bridge I could also indulge in my pleasure in maps, looking at the charts, both the paper version where we made a steady pencil line across the grid and the screen version where, despite the surrounding technology, the names of places still thrilled with possibilities. I do not need to be going to a place to enjoy a map of it – the feat of reducing a three-dimensional world to one that can be folded into your pocket still impresses me after all these years of marvelling at it.

I remember the first time I was set the task of drawing the profile of a range of hills, using the markings of the contour lines on a map. The magic of turning wriggling brown lines that ran across a flat desk into a gently sloping escarpment falling off a sharp cliff was a satisfying pleasure for my ten-year old self, one that has stayed with me. The teacher also got the whole class to learn the symbols on the UK's Ordnance Survey maps, including the difference between the symbol for a church with a spire and that for a church with a tower.

Not that such details were much use out in the more northern reaches of the Atlantic Ocean. There was no spire on the horizon. Up on the bridge watching a cloudless sunset, a fiery orb sinking into the newly inked ocean, spreading fierce orange along the horizon, I had trouble keeping that horizon horizontal as the ship was still rolling. I could hear my father asking why I was taking sunset pictures with the water running down the plughole. We were down to a force 4 wind on the Beaufort scale so I did not have a proper excuse. I took some more pictures, trying to improve my judgement of the roll of the ship against the alignment into thirds of the sky and sea.

~

The watch officer pointed out to me a ship on the horizon, perhaps 12 nautical miles away. That was the second ship we had seen that day, so maybe we would see no ships at all on the next day, as one ship a day did seem to be our appointed ration. The ship currently on the horizon was seriously ugly. We, as a containership, might appear somewhat functional, but the carcarrier was a lump, a boxed lump. Its sides went straight up out of the water and it was topped off by a flat and featureless deck. The watch officer told me carcarriers were floating car parks, layers and layers of cars that are driven in, just like a car park in a big city.

Behind us our corridor of lightly churned water, milky grey, showed us where we had been. The sun came out on the edge of our horizon to spotlight highlights of ocean against the wider and denser greyness. The highlights faded, but the greyness softened too.

~

The layers of the voyage built up. For breakfast we began that first morning with orange juice and then the second morning it was apple juice. We moved on to tomato juice and then grapefruit juice. A thick and sticky mango juice ended the cycle before we came back to orange juice again.

After declining the offer of cold meats, hunks of cheese and various styles of sausages and fried luncheon meat for successive breakfasts, my allotted breakfast place was now laid for me with a jar of marmalade within easy reach. The place for the Man from California was set with a teaspoon waiting for his two spoonfuls of sugar. The two passengers were expected to sit at the foot of the captain's table. Unlike the mail ship from St Helena, as passengers on this ship we were not one of the principal cargoes, we were an adjunct, and with that I felt came an obligation to be interesting, but not difficult.

Mid-voyage and laundry time again. We had a flatter sea under a mostly blue sky with seemingly-innocuous, puffy clouds minding their own business. The messman took me down to the poop deck and showed me the machinery in the laundry room. There was a timetable for who should use the laundry room when and I saw with awkwardness that I was intruding on the time that was set aside for the messman to do all the washing that came with his chores.

I was momentarily confused by the machine labelled, 'For clean clothes only'. Was it in fact a drier, only to be used after the clothes had been washed? No, the messman opened the door and indicated I should put my clothes in there, as opposed to putting them in the washing machine labelled, 'For working clothes' where the greasy, oily overalls and boiler suits attempted to improve their appearance.

The laundry was a small room, sufficient for its task, but having no portholes, so, despite the calmer sea, I took myself back upstairs where I could see a horizon for the half hour of the washing machine doing its thing. Even in the time it took to understand which washing machine was which, the weather had changed, when I was not watching. The occasional wave crested whitely to itself and while the horizon was more or less staying in the same place it did not have the ruler-straight sharpness of the horizon served with breakfast. The sea had gone grey and the grey sea gave way to grey sky in a rather ill-defined way. The greyness sluggishly climbed up beyond the horizon, fumbling further into varying degrees of greyness, none with much conviction.

I decided that my clothes were better transferred from the washing machine to one of the driers, rather than draped prominently over the washlines strung across the laundry room. I somewhat obsessively checked, and double checked, that nothing small of mine was left behind in either the washer or the drier. Heading back to my cabin I met the messman mid-way through his cleaning of the officers' cabins and I confirmed that my laundry was done (so we both knew I was out of the way of him laundering all the week's sheets).

~

For me this was an unusual opportunity to live detached from my normal world for ten days. Ten days carrying no money and no keys and not communicating with the outside world. Life made simple: typing, sleeping and eating, looking out the window alternating with standing outside in the view itself. I set myself a routine which reduced further the number of decisions left to make. Even the range of displacement activities to delay my typing was limited, though the state of the sea gave me a new one, since I allowed myself time off when the sea roughened up.

My laptop was petulantly demanding that I connect to the internet as there were some important things that it thought it should be doing.

My laptop did not like being ignored. The pop-up messages got more strident. There were some really important things that it thought that it really should be doing and then there were some other things that I should absolutely now be doing, no question of reminding later about it. My laptop did not have a box to tick to tell it that there was no internet available and that there was nothing more important for me to be doing than just being in the north Atlantic.

The Man from California was also used to being connected umbilically to the internet, but there were no signals for his phone and there was no internet connectivity, even for his gadgetry. Since I lose internet connectivity in south London when the sun is out and the wi-fi fancies doing something other than talking to my laptop, I had no problem with accepting the reality of not knowing what the outer world was up to. It was harder for the Man from California. He had always known what was going on in California and not knowing was starting to unnerve him.

What did seem strange to me was emerging from several hours' immersion in the inner world of typing up notes about 1940s London, a world entered by going back in my mind to an afternoon in the reading room at the University of Texas, and realising the hum was not of Texan air-conditioning, but the ship's air-conditioning. There would be no walk through the UT campus for a bowl of noodles followed by a bus ride with a bus driver who made whip-cracking noises to entertain the passengers and himself, but instead fried rice, blue cheese sauce and that strange-sounding hybrid of meat and fowl called buffalo chicken wings, with, as an accompanying side dish, the martial arts officer on the importance of reading the classics in each decade of your life.

The classics are, he assured me, like a crystal, as you move through your life so the light shines through them differently. He is Russian and he is seeing Dostoyevsky in a new light on this voyage. I surprised myself by digging out information from my crevices about John Clare when I was at the breakfast table in the B&B in Austin, but I found my crevices to be echoingly empty on the subject of Dostoyevsky. I have read *War and Peace* but I have only read it once and anyway that was one of Tolstoy's, so the wrong Russian.

~

Looking at the crew list in the mess I saw that the captain was seven years older than me, the martial arts officer two years younger than me, the fan of heavy metal was born just before I left school and the industrial music for relaxation comes from a Romanian who spends his days in ear defenders in the engine room. Noticeboards are such interesting places.

While all the ratings are Filipino, the officers are a mix of German, Russian, Slovakian, Filipino and Romanian, so slices of cooked meat and cheese are available at breakfast, lunch and dinner as befits a German-flagged ship, but rice is always there as an alternative to any potato offering, even if rice may seem a little out of place with roast beef.

The routing of the voyage from Wilmington to Antwerp was north, parallel to the coast of the US and Canada, and then east around the coast of Newfoundland, making sure to take a line that was south of the risk of icebergs. After that we would be on several charts that showed no land at all, but those charts would still come from data provided from Taunton in the west of England, where the UK's Hydrographic Office still describes, even if it does not rule, the waves.

English, of a more or less recognisable sort, was the language of the ship, but it was a language of action, a language of command and response. It did not speculate or digress. It was made up of units, not paragraphs. After several days at sea I was thinking, not just speaking, in shorter sentences, reducing my verbs and simplifying my constructions. The martial arts officer had spoken of the deprivation in the isolation of the sea. In my short time aboard there was nothing as blunt as deprivation, but there was simplification, sensory simplification.

One evening, when I had been travelling with my own energy for company for a month, I did shut my cabin door, plug my MP3 player into my laptop and play to the north Atlantic some music from my south London. One of the crew on the way home from St Helena all those years ago had devised an exercise routine from a party-mix cassette she had taped. The routine turned out to be too complicated for the sea conditions. A mixture of crew and passengers had waved their arms or legs to the extent that the ship's motion permitted. Hearing that music brought up a memory of shared laughter. It came from a place that was a long way from where I was. I turned the music off.

The absence was thick. It was not an absence of noise. There was no silence. Things rattled, shook, hummed and throbbed, but there was no noise from the Earth, no birdsong, no children's voices, not even a police siren.

There was absence.

We had joked over the mess table about the overwhelming choice that faces you buying a coffee in the US. On board you could pour more or less coffee into one size of mug. It came with or without milk (one type of milk only, long-life, so I took it without) and with or without sugar. On an ordinary day I do not take sugar so did not check whether the sugar came in any colour other than white.

There was hot water for teabags. There were two types of teabag, the ones the ship supplied that people did not use and Bring Your Own teabags, as one or two did, including the martial arts officer who was scathing about the floor sweepings that filled the teabags in the ship's stores.

On land duplication of items is labelled, with a pejorative sniff, as Redundancy, something to be sacrificed at the altar of Just In Time. At sea for any given action you need a fallback alternative. Just In Time does not work over ten days in the Atlantic. When the computer was not talking to the bridge, it was the weather forecast from the telex machine that the bridge used. (There was a line at the end of the telex transmission about the radio channel to turn to for broadcasts about 'unscheduled storms'.)

Then the galley's washing machine played up. The serious Slovakian chief engineer examined the alterative theories from which to deduce the appropriate tools for an efficacious repair.

Another officer said it was the little green men that have not got anything else to do. They come into the galley to play in the washing machine.

Yet another officer suggested applying a traditional remedy to the washing machine. 'Hit it.'

~

The Man from California and I were invited by the serious Slovakian chief engineer to visit the engine room. It felt like an invitation that required acceptance.

The serious chief engineer told us we move forward because of seven cylinders and one driving shaft. Everything else is serviced by three auxiliary engines. The three auxiliary engines do all the other things that need doing. The chief engineer, while we were still in the relative quietness of the control room, talked about things beyond the engine room door. He talked about types of fuel, that on the high sea we can use higher sulphur, but nearer land we must swap to lower sulphur content. He talked about diesel, about using less fuel if we catch any of the gulf stream or the north Atlantic current. He talked about sludge. He expanded on the subject of categories of rubbish.

Then we put on the most cocooning ear defenders I have ever worn and stepped out into the green and white world of the chief engineer's engine room. We went down and down and down again. Four levels below was the driving shaft itself. It had what looked like a carefully-applied doormat wiping off any excess oil from the shaft. Down this low in the ship there seemed little movement, not like being on the bridge all those decks above.

Down this low did not seem like being at sea. We were in a place where everything was measured, contained, tested and calibrated. Humidity was removed from air. Variables were made steadily constant.

Part way through the tour the chief engineer suggested I would like my picture taken in front of his engine. That felt like a suggestion it would be inappropriate to decline.

There was no doubt the engine room was very well kept. In a collection of photographs of engine rooms this picture could stand with its head held high. The chief engineer liked working with an older vessel. Being launched in 2004, this ship had things that you could see and could mend physically. Newer ships had circuitry on boards that said they were not functioning. Those boards could not be mended. You took the old one out and put the new one in. You did not know what the problem was. You did not solve the problem. There was, for the chief engineer, no satisfaction in putting boards in slots.

The chief engineer had his job, to get us to Europe on time, neither early nor late. We were part of a weekly service and therefore, like the Northern Line in south London, the service needed to be regulated. The gaps between the ships needed to be constant. The weather might not be constant. The sea conditions might not be constant. The loading patterns for the containers would certainly not be constant, but the ships of the service needed to absorb all those variables and turn up when expected. There was a screen on the bridge that showed whether we were delayed or whether we had time to spare for our appointment with the pilot at Antwerp. The chief engineer was the person to bring the figure on that screen down as close to zero as possible. We had been steaming ahead at over 17 knots, but as the screen on the bridge began to show our estimated arrival with more and more time to spare our speed came down, to regulate the service.

The Man from California marvelled at the figures he and the chief engineer exchanged. The Man from California could relate it all to his diesel-fuelled Mercedes back in California. Once past record-player speeds of 33 or 45 rpm I had no revolutions per minute that I could relate to, no benchmark by which to assess whether I should be saying 'Ooh' or 'Aah' on learning that the maximum of the propulsion system driving us was 110 rpm.

I could appreciate the shadow boards with all the tools neatly hanging in their allotted places. I could see a well-signed eyewash station and watch everyone in the engine room wearing their ear defenders. The order and systems were visible to me. I could smile and nod, but questions did not come to me as easily in the deeper places of the engine room as they did on the bridge, where we looked out to where we were going, not how we were going to get there.

A watchkeeper had told me how navigation and watchkeeping were much older than the engines and engineers in the bottom of the ship. An engineer had told me that the engine room was where the real work was done.

The captain offered the chief engineer his black bread at breakfast. The chief engineer took his slice of cheese after the captain. Each of them gave the other, and their differing jobs, respect.

We ascended steadily and came out into the light and the air.

After only an hour deep below in the self-contained world of the engine room I was happy to be back in daylight, back with the variables that I understood better, even if they were less capable of control.

The reality of typing myself into a pattern was a comfortable way of being. It fitted with the patterns of working all around me. In Austin I had found that the rhythm of my days fell naturally into five or six hours of reading, resulting in about five or six pages of notes. As I typed up those Austin notes on board ship I found that a day was of five or six typing hours, though, unlike the watchkeepers, I had the luxury that more could be pushed into one day or I could allow the sea conditions to be an excuse to let myself off with fewer hours on another day.

Outside of that came planning, whether for the structure of the next day's typing or starting to think what might be the options for the next trip (Iceland prefaced by side trips to Oxford and Birmingham). The practicalities of life also hung around, wanting attention, but the point of main effort was typing and getting the best from my time on board, a time which would not come again.

~

There were four cabins that could take passengers and the captain told me that in the summer there was usually at least one passenger for each transatlantic leg.

I only rarely caught a glimpse of the Man from California outside the mess, perhaps making his way on a walk up and down and around the ship as his exercise. He told me he was not yet in summer cycling shape and he did not have walking knees. He was certainly more substantially built than me and ventured out to walk at times when I kept to the internal staircases for going up and down. One evening he timed the return journey from the top of the ship's roll, down through the trough, up to other side and back again: 12 seconds.

The seas were calmer than those first days after leaving Wilmington, but I remained acutely conscious all voyage that the route to the bow was hidden from view, under the containers, and the bow itself was not visible from the bridge. I remembered hearing the writer and traveller Nicholas Crane speak about the importance of knowing when to turn back, about the dangers of having a fixed goal in mind and how those dangers are magnified by a rigid timetable.

One mealtime the Man from California brought with him the topic of collisions at sea and deaths. Not a topic that I chose to spend time developing with him. The captain replied with a few shorter sentences. We moved on.

The containership was not a place for fussing. The risks are labelled. The signs are there to be read. People get on with their job and assume, until the contrary is proved, that you will get on with your job.

There were all sorts of policies and procedures on laminated cards, on walls, on noticeboards. One warned at some length of the quadratic squat effect. The short version of the warning appeared to be not of the dangers of certain gym exercises but that you should not travel at speed in a canal unless you want your bow to sink beneath the self-created wave. The policies were all in English but were more prone to exclamation marks than the lawyer in me would expect. Danger of death would, in the world I am from, be a factual statement, undiluted by multiple exclamation marks.

One of the noticeboard procedures itemised those things that the watch officer must contact the ship's captain about. They included 'a list for no obvious reason'. I liked the idea of alerting a higher authority to an occurrence of pointless bureaucracy. No list should be made without a reason for it. Reasons may be of two types: a good reason or the real reason. The real reason need not be publically disclosed, but it must be privately distinguished from the good (and given) reason and it may or may not have other adjectives attached.

I come back to earth, or rather to sea. Of course if the ship lists to one side without an obvious reason the captain should be alerted. In fact I suspect the chances are everyone would be alerted by a severe list, even if there was an obvious reason.

Another notice released a volley of exclamation marks about the correct procedure for getting updated Notices to Mariners and chart revisions. Ah, the romance of the sea – version control of documentation.

In one of my breaks from the keyboard I was back on deck, looking up to the skies, made up of medium-sized blue patches and for the first time on the voyage I saw a plane's contrail, passing us as they too navigated to Europe using great circle navigation. Like us they were not pushing themselves out into the utter emptiness of the open seas for any longer than navigational sense required. The shortest distance between two points was not the shorter line that I saw on a flat map, the curve of a globe making the world smaller than that. The planeload above me would be home in time for lunch tomorrow. I would be home in time for dinner, but several days hence.

That plane may have a moving map, there, at the touch of a finger, in the back of each passenger's seat. On that map the space between the two continents, between America and Europe, is just one label, a blue absence of anything. When you are on that blue absence, the charts have many more names. Each day as I looked at our pencilled line across the chart of the day, we passed new names. Flemish Cap sounded quite light-hearted as a name, whereas when we came to the Faraday Fracture that sounded much more serious. Nearer to home there was the oddly out of place Porcupine Bank.

Wrapped within a full set of layered clothes, I watched the wind pushing us on this the 'downhill' run, the voyage back to Europe. There were flecks of white across the ocean, but at the moment those were merely decorative, with no urgency to them.

Back to my keyboard and the Romanian music in my corridor was more lyrical than the metal stop and start of the weekday music. It was Saturday afternoon, the afternoon beyond a morning of work. There were some violins, a piano accordion was building up crescendos and a singer believed deeply in whole sentences.

I had my diary with me, but it was entirely empty of any commitments. It had nowhere to be and no expectation of who or what might be there. I marked in it how long I had taken to type how much. It was an indicator of quantity and speed, not of quality, but in this vastness I needed some markers, some pattern for my progression.

After one morning of typing up 4,000 words of notes, I allowed myself the luxury of timeless wake-watching, mesmerised by the patterns as the propeller churned within the outline of the whitened water that left the sides of the ship's hull as we passed through our self-set corridor. The clouds hinted that there might be some blue behind them.

I was on board a containership, watching the ocean, savouring the moment and bottling its essence for more pressured times.

I was also travelling by keyboard between the Austin of a few weeks earlier and mid 20th century London.

In one particular now, the one on board a containership, we were getting nearer England. The German captain teased me that the sea will be grey. The sky will be grey. Our weather will now be English summer weather. All will be grey. Soon we will move our last hour forward and I will be ahead of myself, because Antwerp time is one hour ahead of the time in south London.

6

A cold start to summer

I was ahead of my home time zone. I had typed up all the notes I had made in the Texan reading room and added thoughts of my own. I had 27,000 words of typing, more than 40 pages of typing, saved on my laptop, backed up on a memory stick. I had updated my lists and revised my planning schedules.

I was ready for the next instalment.

However we were still moving steadily towards the English Channel, our speed slowed down to 14 knots to make sure that we did not arrive too early for our appointment with the Antwerp pilot.

We were still at sea, still living the seafarers' life. I was still detached from the life that I call normal life. As I wrote that I realised that the question of what would be normal for me in my writing year was yet to be tested. I left my job towards the end of March and got on the plane to Austin in early April so now in May I have not yet begun to create what will be normal for me in my writing year. I have not yet begun to put into practice my ideas on how I will inhabit the space I have given myself.

The Man from California, after a week, had decided that travelling by sea on a containership was a wonderful experience he would not have missed, but there were several buts. He looked forward to the clocks staying still. He looked forward to meal times of his own choosing. A week was long enough. Two weeks was too much of a good thing.

After more than a week at sea I had built a normal for my voyaging self, but with the sea having had more lumpy days than times of unvarying flatness, I had not taken possession of what I had thought would have been my regular walk, a lap of the ship. If I had been writing a novel then I could have taken a leap of imagination and landed, regardless of sea conditions, out in the bow, brushing in details from talking to others. If I was a proper Traveller (with a capital T) I would have gone to the bow and back by day and by night, in rough seas and in calm, with a range of confident adverbs. Instead I have been out to the bow once in company on the safety tour and once on my own. Yes I have only once taken myself out into the silence, detached from even the detachment of life on board.

Going out to a place where the noise of the engine had faded, where the clattering of the vibrations was still, I was smaller than usual. I no longer had a name. I was a speck on a dot in the ocean, listening to nothing.

I concentrated on that nothing and began to itemise what nothing sounded like. There was a water swish under the bow as we purposed ever forward. The deck where I was standing was roofed, making a sounding chamber for the faintest of groans. It was the slow and low pain of the containers groaning. A sound that was barely there, but deeply unhappy, a wordless misery, like someone beyond help.

It was only once that I heard the containers. For the rest of the time I was where the engine vibrated, where I was the passenger in the Supercargo cabin, where my exercise was limited and I could begin to understand the caging effect of being on board, carried along for unyielding months at a time. Four or five months at sea was the usual length of contract, but extensions were not uncommon. I spoke to one crew member now on his ninth month on this contract, going round and round the Atlantic.

Globalisation was a word that came to be bandied about in the closing years of the 20th century. It was seen as a noun released by the forces of deregulation and that may have been when it came to be more widely visible, but the unit of globalisation, the physical thing that started to make it possible, was the container. It was back in the 1960s that the practical arguments were settled, first about the sizes of containers and then about the nature of the fittings to enable a standard-sized container to be lifted and moved in any port. Once those decisions had been made it mattered not what language was spoken in the port, only that the port had the necessary cranes and lifting devices.

In ports now there is a lot to be done in a short time. Ports are not places of rest and relaxation for crew members. The port, wherever it may be, has not only fences, but also distance, separating it from land-based activities. Walking off a ship just to buy a newspaper or a pint (whether of fresh milk or of beer) is not possible. Shore leave is not a given every time a ship berths, but at least on this size ship they do berth. The crew see dry land even if they do not always stand on it. The largest oil tankers are too big for all but Rotterdam of the conventional ports. They lie offshore in one part of the world taking on oil and then when day and night have alternated for long enough and the tankers have moved to another part of another ocean, they lie offshore and discharge the oil into pipes or other, smaller ships.

In my time on the containership I glimpsed a complete, but other, world that my own life is dependent on. Some worlds are important to those who live in them, but do not impinge on those of us living outside that world. This, the seafaring world, is different. It supports the consuming society I live in and the consuming society knows it not.

~

There were signs that we were nearing port. We saw gannets again, straight-winged, black tips to their wings and head, with their necks stained a nicotine-yellow. (A non-smoker like me knows about nicotine stains? Well I started work in the days when there were no people sneaking out for a cigarette break, because in those, now far off days, they smoked at their desk, for those were the days when an ashtray was an office stationery item.) At breakfast I had tried to demonstrate to the Man from California how far up the wingtip the gannet's black went. (He was missing his internet, the being able to look things up as he thought of them.) He asked whether the black stretched up the gannet's wing like opera gloves in historical times. I replied it was less than that. I had in mind just the tips dipped in a paint pot to do a small job of touching up a scrape, but, looking at the gannets again, I thought the black tips were perhaps nearer to evening glove length.

In addition we had some ordinary seagulls circling the ship. Or, perhaps to be more geometrically correct, ovalling the ship?

We were getting closer to port. The paperwork was increasing. All crew and passengers have to declare relevant contents on a schedule. The lawyer in me turned the piece of paper over and back, looking for a definition of *relevant* or indeed an explanation of what counted as *contents*. The passenger in me looked at what the crew had declared and noted down which of those things I had too: laptop, watch, camera, MP3 player, e-book reader, mobile phone. I scheduled out the baggage of my early 21st century.

There was an inventory to be drawn up of the things entering the port on the ship that would be staying on the ship. The list noted 20 fridges, three laminators, one flat iron and one ironing board. Foodstuffs were measured out onto the list by the kilo: 25 kg of coffee and 16,000 teabags. Can I have read that correctly? Is that why nearly everyone drinks coffee? Did some cook order teabags long ago that were the cheapest of the cheap, perhaps even, as the martial arts officer thought, teabags filled from the floor sweepings left over after all else had been cleared away? Even if there were 20 crew members using three teabags a day that would keep them all going for more than eight months of tea-drinking.

I had scarcely dented the supplementary supplies I had bought in Wilmington. I gave to the martial arts officer the lemon and ginger teabags. He thanked me. He told me he would not refuse a present from an English lady. (I had been eating my meals with both elbows on the table in an effort to stabilise the eating process on rougher sea days. Not the look of an English lady.) His own supplies of teabags were low so he was very happy to accept a present of more teabags and the lemon and ginger teabags he would save for his early watch. They are, he assures me, good teabags for waking up.

Those supplementary supplies also included what I had learnt to call crackers. I offered those to the Man from California who had a train journey from Antwerp to Amsterdam in the morning. Somehow I am offering him a box of his favourites and he too was happy to take on my surplus, as supplementary supplies of his own for the onward journey.

During my evenings at sea I had read the book with the backdrop of a road trip from New Jersey to Chicago and I offered it to the German captain. He had told me earlier in the voyage that he began reading books in English some 15 years ago because he could tell that the German translations he had been reading, were lacking. The other book I had bought in Wilmington, the book about Emily Dickinson's correspondence, was heavy-going. (Maybe it would be more suited to a German translation.) I did not offer the captain Emily Dickinson.

The continuum that had been my time at sea, that state of having no obligations, other than to not get in the way, was cut. Re-entry loomed. For one more day I was still a spectator. The fan of heavy metal music confirmed the booking for me of a taxi from the port of Antwerp. After that I would be making decisions again.

The Man from California reconnected to what had been going on in California. Crew members throughout the ship were on their mobile phones, taking advantage of the strengthening signals as we made our way along the crowded highway of the English Channel, keeping to the traffic separation lanes, watching for the small fishing boats, straying from their inshore area, bobbing about in the force 5 wind that we were big enough not to notice.

We did roll enough to set my shower curtain off again, opening and closing, rings gossiping on the curtain rail. It was a sound that had my ears straining to work out what it was when it started on the first night. By the end of the voyage the sound went into the unheard background.

The shower curtain had a pattern of green waves and arcs of seabirds that looked like the ocean when I first saw it. Now I had seen the ocean and the ocean was grey and black and blue, turning green only when we came nearer to land. It was only then that the seabirds came back to see us. The shower curtain was, I decided, patterned like coastal waters, seen from the land.

After days of perhaps one ship a day and that one only far out on the horizon, our space felt invaded with ships to the left and right, ahead and behind. All around were ships being sucked in to the Dover Straits, all heading in the same direction, before they splintered off, each to its different port and its own berth.

The Dover Straits are, along with the Malacca Straits and the South China Seas, the busiest shipping areas, I was told repeatedly by crew members as they passed me, busy with their own preparations for the voyage down river into the port of Antwerp. I was down to the last handful of my own voyage of 3,570 nautical miles. The sky had roused itself to a pale blue, with dissipating contrails. The visibility had improved, after early morning mist, shrouding everything outside our two-mile bubble, testing my ability to cut out my worrying engine for things that I can do nothing about.

The day passed. Ships passed. The pilot came on board. The engine tone changed. Down on the poop deck I was looking for a sunset, wondering what I might find for a suitable foreground, but the sun faded, without visibly setting. The time for such things had passed. I was glad I had taken the first opportunity to photograph a north Atlantic sunset, the fiery orb that I can take out of order when I re-arrange my photographs to show others. It will make a suitable ending for the voyage.

~

The last breakfast was like the first supper, just me and the Man from California.

Then it was time to reverse my arrival on board in Wilmington. Again I waited in the deck office. This time the safe was unlocked. My passport was handed back to me.

A taxi was announced. A boiler-suited Filipino seaman took my suitcase down the steep and oily gangway.

It was not raining so I did ask the taxi driver to take a picture of me, disembarking from what had turned out to be a good idea.

The taxi driver then established that I was not from California and therefore I was not his passenger. The immigration procedure for an American is different from the procedure for a European, even one from Britain with its anomalies outside the Schengen area.

The taxi driver rang his office. My taxi was on its way. The taxi driver went back to the gangway and this time gathered up the Man from California instead.

The driver who was not my taxi driver made a second call to his office before he drove off.

I stood alongside the gangway, once more watching fork-lift trucks on steroids. This time I was watching the port operations of, I think the captain said, the third biggest of the Continental ports. This time the trucks were scooting around, tidying up the offloadings from what I now thought of as 'my' containership.

From high above the captain spotted me and called down.

I was not alone.

Then a taxi pulled up. I got into the taxi and into another opportunity to see someone else's normal. He drives for two days and then has five days of vacation to spend with his mother who is 97 and lives just beyond the port. He worked for a big multi-national when it was eating small companies. He was busy on computers, sitting on a chair in an office that made numbers. Then the government and the multi-national had a programme to pay him to sit on a chair at home and not sit on the chair in the office anymore. He had two wives, but now he is 72 and does not have a wife. Now he has a job where he speaks to different people every day he works and he goes to a different place every day he works. He uses his languages. His own language is a luxury. He speaks French because people south of Brussels speak French and he speaks English because that is the language of the economy, that is the language the world speaks.

Today Antwerp is full with a conference so he is working an extra day. Brussels airport has a baggage handlers strike. The ring road around Antwerp leads to Brussels (and to everywhere) so it is always busy.

His mother was rushed into hospital at the weekend. She is stronger now. She is in a normal room now. It is quiet when she is not in her house. He cries because he is afraid it will be quiet always in her house.

I sit very still in the passenger seat. I wonder who else he has spoken to about his mother's illness and his own fears, the intimations of mortality. It was a 25-minute journey to Antwerp airport. The land should be firm and definite, but the sea was still moving under me. I was back in my known world of land-based activity but I had not caught up with myself. I offered up some phrases to the taxi driver that I hoped sounded sympathetic, even in his third language. I have not got quite the balance of my land legs.

We moved on to speak of practicalities. The taxi driver asked if I am for the private plane or the public plane. I confirmed it was the airport terminal for commercial planes, for public planes that I wanted.

Once inside the correct airport terminal, the representative at the airline counter showed me how I could save many euros on my flight home, by not catching the next flight to London.

~

I am in a time of waiting, waiting for the flight after next, the flight that goes to London for a more sensible price. I am accompanied in my waiting at Antwerp airport by drills from the airport's building work.

The contented humming of marine machinery has faded. I have left that time, in its present tense, behind, but it is a time that

I will always take with me, that time of being at sea in May, a gift from 2013.

~

Five days after I left the port of Antwerp, the sea still rocked me at the moment before waking and then that reminder too had gone.

A lack of vibration became normal again – instead of a worry about why the engines might have stopped.

I am on dry land. I have finished the travelling that I planned many months before. Now what?

Now I am working out what to do and how to do it. I have set myself a summer in south London at the keyboard.

On my return from Antwerp I re-entered life in London, but this was not my accustomed life, bounded by the electronic red eye blinking with unread work emails from across time zones, this was a new project.

I had a simple enough project plan: 12 chapters of (give or take) 7,000 words. Adding a bibliography, permissions and acknowledgements to that would bring together somewhere between 80,000 and 100,000 words, making more than 250 pages, which would be enough to count as a Proper Book. I planned to draft and redraft that several times over, on screen and on paper, by the end of the calendar year. Then I would be ready to swing into the production phase and move into the world resembling that of annual report production, known from my day job.

I had spent some time musing on the Northern Line, before I left for Austin. (Musing tends to be my default activity when standing up on a crowded tube train.) I had mused up a list of 12 chapter headings and I had mused through each chapter's possible content.

I set out those Northern Line chapter headings ready to receive the material I had found in the Texan reading room. At sea I typed my way steadily through the Austin material, slotting it tidily under those headings. Some of the choices of where to put which item were somewhat arbitrary, but while at sea I typed everything, perhaps temporarily, into a home.

Now the land had stopped moving, the plan was to build out each chapter in turn. I was no longer on expedition, gathering material. I came face to face with the reality of typing. No amount of ideas in the abstract could be mistaken for an actual book. Part paragraphs jotting down some thoughts arising from the raw material I had captured in Austin were just that – parts of an incomplete whole.

An actual book requires doing, systematic and disciplined doing, day by day, a structured application to the mechanics of creation, whether or not the view from the keyboard feels particularly inspiring. Ethereal images may float down from somewhere quite else, but they will drift off again, leaving a vague sense of loss, if not caught in words, working away at the job in hand.

I tell myself I can do being disciplined. Diligence could be my middle name (if it began with a W).

The project plan was simple.

To go from the plan to its execution, each morning I got up with my alarm set as it was when I was commuting into central London. Instead of embarking on the Northern Line I had the luxury of a proper coffee and around 7.30am I embarked on some more typing. I stop at some point for a second coffee. Most mornings become the afternoon before I declare lunch. The idea of stopping for lunch may come to mind at 12.30pm, at the same time as some other ideas come to mind, and then it is 1.30pm and I realise I had meant to stop and by 2.30pm I decide I really must just make a note of the next idea and leave it dangling while I take a break and have some actual, rather than thought of, lunch.

London did an impersonation of summer in early May while I was away from it. Now I am back and in the cold. It could be November. The daylight is weak and insipid, damp with recent rain. There is no risk of being lured into a chair in the garden when I do eventually break for lunch.

One swallow does not make a summer, but I wonder what three swifts do, as they scythe, fiercely stiff-winged, through the south London air, set in their purpose, on their way to somewhere more congenial. I put a second fleece on to go outside and impose some, transient, order on the weeds patterning my patio, before coming back inside to the warmth and some afternoon weeding of my inboxes.

Each morning I have afresh the pleasure of typing some words that have never before been typed in that particular order. Hours pass while I leave the present of cold, damp London and go back to April in Austin or May at sea, to the unexpectedly visible history of Wilmington or the harder-nosed modernity of Charlotte. I am immersed in the moment, at the keyboard, typing (and saving and backing up and saving again).

This is my writing year: me and the keyboard and words.

The typed words begin to add up. Chapters expand into thousands of words. A further chapter is added to another chapter. Not that there is merit in quantity on its own, but without words typed there can be no merit at all. Volume is a starting point, something to edit and rearrange.

Sitting admiring the perfection of a blank page is not for me. The ideal adjective may remain loose, running free, just beyond my reach, but I can still make a beginning. I take a subject with a verb and add an object. If (when I am out looking for something completely else), if then the ideal adjective does calm down and come quietly to heel, then I will have somewhere made ready to receive that once missing and unfettered adjective.

When I meet friends in the evening to recount traveller's tales, I know that the less exotic days of staying still, the days that did not provide stories, are the ones that will make a difference this year. Gathering all the raw material, enjoying the observation of the less usual, of the mildly improbable, all that was well and good, but without time to reflect and digest and time to capture it on the page, the raw material and the observation would be just the side product of a holiday, albeit an unusual one.

Before I set off on my travels to Austin I had agreed with myself that if the writing, the typing, the getting words down, frozen, with all their limitations onto paper, was not something that I enjoyed then that would be fine. I would go back, sooner than originally planned, to the corporate world. I would have tried out the reality of the idea of 'one day I might write a book'. I would have brought 'one day' forward.

On the transatlantic voyage the martial arts officer had told the

Man from California and me a joke from the Soviet era.

A small clerk in a small office, 'I dream of going to Paris again.'

Fellow worker, 'I did not know you went to Paris.'

Clerk replies, 'I did not go to Paris. I had a dream before of going to Paris.'

I knew it was quite possible I would put my foot through my dream and tear it, but I had decided to go there. (Not, I hasten to add, to Paris. That would not be my choice of destination. I got stuck in Paris once for work for three weeks in August with only the clothes for the originally planned three days. Everywhere that was open made no secret of wanting to be shut. The transaction I originally went to Paris for did, eventually, complete. Happily I do not remember the delay's details, apart from a fire in the office's electrical cupboard, but it is a Saturday afternoon in Giverny, my treat of a detour to the gardens where Monet painted, that stays with me.)

Plenty of people on hearing of my writing plans had spoken about them in emotional terms, straying into language I would not use: living the dream, following your heart, pursuing your passion.

Dreams and hearts and passions, on display, visible, in a public place?

Oh dear me, I think not.

I am planning to write a book. The plan is a book with a number of words (which does not make it literary. That might presume a category of merit and I am wary of presumptions and generalisations). The plan is to put those words on a physical page because it is my book so I can be old-fashioned if I want to.

Executing that plan of a book will give me the excuse to do some things I have always fancied doing and will give me the impetus to try some things that I might not otherwise.

It is nothing more than that.

Well it is a little more than that. It is two books. The Proper Book: the book I left my job to write, the one about places associated with Louis MacNeice, the poet whose words I have enjoyed for more than thirty years.

And then this book.

Though this book has the luxury (if I want it to) of starting a new paragraph with an *and*, it would be misleading to call this book the Improper Book. No raciness here. This book will require as much discipline as the Proper Book. It will also get drafting and redrafting time, with standing and leaving time in between. This book is my book, rather than MacNeice's. It is some of the bottled essence of my writing year: the ebbs and flows of capturing the raw material of now, moulding it into shapes as now passes out of immediate view and then tightening the words that make up those shapes so they will be strong enough to go out on their own.

Sending my words out on their own is something I will have to get used to.

When I got back from Antwerp so many wanted to know about my travels that I decided it was time to do a newsletter, telling folks some of what I had been doing since I took off for Austin. Being a foreigner in the land of blogs and tweets and certainly not an inhabitant of facebookland, I (not being a child of the 21st century) opted for a newsletter, since letter-writing, even though these days my paragraphs travel more often by email than by post, is something native to me.

I typed the newsletter. I put it to one side, for some standing and leaving in between time. I pulled together a distribution list of those I thought might be interested in reading some stories of my travelling with the poetry of Louis MacNeice.

Then I had to face the difficult bit: pressing the send button.

The newsletter words were not functional words. They were not board minutes, not a corporate governance report, not impersonal words. The words in the newsletter were my personal words about what I had been doing. Although I was not broadcasting them out to the entire ether in a public blog, but only emailing them to a selected few who had a pre-existing interest in my doings, they were my words going out on their own.

Intellectually of course I had known since before I started typing either book that sending my words out on their own was ultimately what this year was all about. Depositing in the UK's copyright libraries a book written by me that unmet others might read or, nearer to home, that my sister's children might one day take a look at, was the point of writing a book (or two).

Sending the words of my newsletter out was the first step towards achieving that. It also made me realise some of what would be involved, for me, in putting my words out there on their own, perhaps even passions and dreams becoming visible in a public place.

I pressed the send button.

Then I went out for a walk round the block, in the damp daylight, and got cold and wet feet from misjudging a puddle jump and landing on a pivoting paving slab.

~

Having friends in various time zones makes meeting up difficult (not that having coffee on a whim is practical with most of my London-based friends either) but I did have the benefit of several of them reading my newsletter during my night and the next morning I had replies with encouraging enthusiasm attached.

I could, for four pages anyway, write in a way that my readers (pre-selected as they were) enjoyed. That was a start. Not perhaps full justification for writing two whole books, but it was a start.

~

So May moved on into June. The weather in London got no better. What the radio's weather forecast glossed over as 'rain showers', lingered for several hours and made the whole afternoon drippingly wet. This did have the silver lining that I was not getting distracted by sunlight. I was not closing the blinds to shut out the glare, but I was still looking out over my flat roof, continuing to see birds that were new, not to me, but new to me at home in south London. A pied woodpecker tested out a neighbour's overgrown conifers, startling some starlings. A rather scrawny goldfinch came to visit for several days, pecking the rainwater puddles on my flat roof. Sparrows made those puddles a regular calling place, their chirping cheerful, despite the weather, but not something that could be elevated to the title of birdsong.

Fledging blue tits tried out their wings. One discovered that aquilegias are decorative and their stems are elegantly slender, but they are insufficiently structural to hold up even the weight of a young blue tit. He made instead for a more substantial shrub, a flowering broom, itself just beginning to think about the flowering part of its name, despite the chill in the air. A sibling blue tit could not make up her mind. She came close to approaching the washline and, moments from touchdown, decided better of it, veering off for something of a crash-landing in my rose bush. By tomorrow (certainly) and by this afternoon (probably) both will have mastered this flying lark, but just at the moment, it did not seem at all obvious, and I allowed myself the displacement activity of worrying for them.

Time was for me no longer measured in electronic red blinking eyes; but instead there was the morning for typing, the afternoon for chores and the evening for being sociable, unless I chose to invert or reverse or even abandon the three-session plan, which I could, since it was my writing year of my rules for my books.

After several days of Proper Book writing I put that to one side and did some days of writing this book. When the previous chapter of the Proper Book had stood for long enough it was time to print it out (on pieces of old-fashioned paper) for reading afresh and for redrafting.

After the redrafting I had a clearer idea of what that chapter was actually about, as opposed to what I had mused on the Northern Line, months ago, that it might be about, so I updated my chapter outline – another of my working lists – accordingly.

Two drafts of a chapter of the Proper Book later and a standing period had passed for the most recently written chapter of this book, so time to swop back over to this book and this chapter.

There are courses on how to write and how not to, but for once I had decided not to read the instruction book. I had decided to plunge into getting first-hand experience. I was taking a slightly indirect route through June, making up my own zig-zag as I went along from chapter to chapter, between the two books.

I have always had more than one book on the go as a reader, so why not as a writer?

No doubt there are many good reasons why not, but being ignorant of what received wisdom says I can not do, I am free to do it anyway, writing two books at the same time. That gives me variety in my working day, but a variety that is focused on the point of main effort, book writing. Even the most skittish piece of admin gets corralled into its lower place. It will get attention, but later in the day, after the morning energy has burst into writing.

Some of my Proper Book raw material was fitting conveniently into my mused Northern Line chapter headings and some just would not, so I popped it into a document I labelled Cold Storage, a place to keep things that might come in handy later, things that it seemed unwise to throw out this soon, when I did not know what I might find as I travelled through the later months of this writing year. (I do prefer having a backup reserve available, whether of clean socks or improbable ponderings.)

Where to put marginalia – a much grander term than mere scribblings? There were several references to marginalia in Austin. Are notes somehow elevated if they are made to the left or right, in the margins, whereas notes in the body of the text are relegated to the status of mere amendments, prosaic marks of the working day? I wanted to find a home for those thoughts, but they did not fit into either book's Austin chapter, so into Cold Storage they went (along with the lead story in a magazine for sale in Austin airport about turkey shooting, 'Never miss a gobbler again'). Phrases sent to sit in a corner, waiting for their time which might never come, waiting to be picked for the team.

As I redrafted the redraftings I knew there were some phrases, some cul-de-sacs, that came into the category of William Faulkner's much-quoted advice to 'kill your darlings'. Sometimes there are glorious passages that sparkle too much for where they are. They need to be excised and, if not finally killed, at least plunged into Cold Storage. Sometimes there are interesting detours, but on a second rereading I face up to what I could see on the first rereading, they are a detour too far, they take the reader more than three steps from the main route, so off they too must go into Cold Storage.

These are my books so I do look up from time to time as I am writing them. As I learnt from my father when taking photographs, I look around me, bending my knees, leaning in or out, not forgetting to look at the view behind. There are plenty of different angles to watch for, even as I progress in the general direction of the mused chapter outlines. Detours are an integral part of where I am going. It is just that sometimes, even I know the detour has diverted too far and it would not be fair to leave the reader, looking out over my flat roof, worrying about the frailty of fledging blue tits, when I have already, on a whim, gone off to Oxford to drink some coffee and do some observing, in the name of research.

~

While the basic idea was to come back to dry land to type through the summer, I had some side trips in mind. I knew that some of the chapters would benefit from a site visit. Calling such visits 'research trips' might be too grand a term, but some time away from the keyboard would do my summer and the books some good. They would be time to do some MacNeiceing and to see some more of the daylight, the sunlight even, that I wanted from this writing year.

MacNeice read classics at Oxford and had his first job in Birmingham. Oxford and Birmingham were places I would enjoy revisiting so they went onto the visiting list.

I had considered various possible ways of structuring my writing about MacNeice, but came to the conclusion that a chronological underpinning was the best. A timeline that put Oxford earlier than Birmingham, the undergraduate student before the assistant lecturer, was obvious and there are times when obvious is best. Chronology is a loadbearing structure. It can carry weight. Fancy bits can be added for fun on the side.

I hasten to add that I am not planning to go everywhere MacNeice went (not least because of my time constraints). I plan to pick and choose those places that interest me for a writing visit. I already know that visiting for a holiday is visiting for relaxation, which is not the same as visiting for writing.

So bearing all that in mind I went off to Oxford in June for a writing visit.

My first stop in Oxford had to be Blackwell's. I know there are other famous bookshops, with both character and a long history, but Blackwell's is still for me The Bookshop, the one prefaced by the definitive definite article. It had been The Bookshop for me when, as a teenager, I first entered it, the very home of all known learning itself.

There was the Norrington Room, dug out deeper than the level of a mere basement, containing a rollcall of all the categories there were of knowledge, while, ascending to the floors above, I could enter the realms of imagination and unsubstantiated possibility, where things became more speculative.

There, as in the bookshops in Wilmington and in Austin, I could still find what I was not looking for, before I emerged blinking once more into the daylight.

I sat in a coffee shop in Oxford, listening out for stories. 'Can you test me on schizophrenia?' asked one table. From the waiting queue came the aggrieved tones of self-justification, 'She says so, but I don't remember kissing her friend.'

Coffee shops were not places I went to as a student, but then coffee was different then. Back in the 1980s more advanced students had a percolator with a filter in the top into which they poured ground coffee bought from a special shop, but I boiled a kettle and poured hot water over instant granules (or converged with others on someone else's room where they did the same).

I spent my student days further east than Oxford, so walking around Oxford was not walking around my university days. I was a tourist, on the outside, observing, and having observed, I headed off home.

Sitting in stationary traffic in the midst of shops on Oxford's outskirts, only just beginning the journey home, I saw a young girl, no more than four, looking longingly at her most favourite thing of the moment. Her wise grandmother realised that pulling her charge along would not get her home any faster so, as the wind blew through this unseasonable June, she tightened her sari and let her granddaughter come closer to the object of her attentions. The little girl reached out her small hand, glancing back at her grandmother for approval. The man in leathers astride his motorbike, waiting for his passenger to finish in the shops had, I was sure, got some expression on his face, but not one we could see as his head was encased in a matt black crash helmet.

He leant the motorbike slightly towards the little girl and she stroked its vivid lime-green paintwork.

I suspected that the matt black crash helmet chose a lime-green motorbike to turn heads and, although not his target audience, the turning of a small but appreciative head would still have brightened an otherwise grey and uninviting afternoon.

~

The 19th century Scottish essayist (made grumpy by what might have been stomach ulcers) Thomas Carlyle said that, 'The greatest university of all is a collection of books' and one of the many things that he did in his life was contribute to the foundation of the London Library in 1841. As part of my writing year I treated myself to membership of the London Library which entitled me to borrow up to ten books at a time from the one million available in, they said, fifty languages.

One of the library's founding principles, that is still followed today, is that no book should ever be discarded, no matter how idiosyncratic or unfashionable it becomes, which made it an ideal place to find books I had on my list for MacNeice purposes and books I did not.

Being tucked into a corner of St James' Square in the West End of London the London Library does not have the cheap noodle options for lunch that the reading room in Austin did, but when London does get around to having some summer weather there will be the garden in the centre of St James' Square for picnicking and until then bowls of warming soup are on offer in various of the sandwich shops nearby.

The London Library spreads in opportunistic fashion over three buildings, which are partially-interconnected. Not having a sense of direction I navigated my way by reference to the colour of the floor covering. In one part the lino was green. In another area one of the staircases had sumptuous red carpet on the floor and distinguished writers lining the walls. There were so many of them that they went up, not only as far as the Gentlemen, but beyond that, to the more remote Ladies Lavatory.

I did wonder about the inclusion of the word Lavatory with respect to the Ladies and its omission with respect to the Gentlemen, but then again Gentlemen is a long word, filling on its own all the available space on the wooden plaque.

I did also wonder about the lack of apostrophes, but that is only one of a number of idiosyncrasies the London Library has to offer the new member. The Library's classification system is not Dewey, the one I have known from childhood, but a shelfmark system all of their own devising. There is Literature and then there is the different category of Fiction. The membership pack comes with a reminder of certain rules and expected etiquette. It does not mention the advisability of wearing flat shoes in parts of Literature and neighbouring categories. Or at least any heels worn should be substantial ones, to walk with ease the floors that resemble fire escape gratings.

Looking for books about a specific place gave me practice in trying to not get lost as I navigated between the bookstacks of History and those of Topography.

The focus of the library is on the humanities, so the Science section in particular has some strange neighbours within it, 'Suffrage, Submarine, Sticks (walking)'. I was making my way to Radio at the time and so did not let myself be diverted to see how many books there were about Sticks (walking). Even after a few visits I could see how I would easily find books on what I was not looking for. When I was looking for Finance (relating to recent times in Iceland) that too was to be found in Science. It was after passing Fire and Finger Print, before the category of Ferns. Such a method allows the application of the principle, it was suggested, of productive browsing.

The London Library is a place that has gradually accumulated. It is not exactly old-fashioned (I write these words sitting at a small table in Fiction next to a broadband router and other members too are settled in their favourite spots, pecking at their laptops), but neither is the library fully of the world outside its doors.

I have the luxury of heading home, away from central London before the rush hour and as I walked through St James' Square I saw the memorial for Yvonne Fletcher, which jolted me back to harsher times. Yvonne Fletcher was a police officer in 1984 policing a demonstration outside the Libyan embassy in St James'

Square when she was shot dead by someone within the embassy. Back in 1984 London was a foreign place to me. It was where news happened. There was a picture of police helmets lying untidily on the ground, shocking to the proper order of things.

A bowler hat strode past me. I can not think that I had ever before seen a bowler hat being worn in the ordinary course of the wearer's life. From time to time bowler hats come out for ceremonial occasions, but this seemed to be a hat that the wearer put on to keep his head warm and dry. He hurried on for a late appointment.

After many years of living in London there is still plenty that is foreign to me about London. When on the transatlantic voyage I was discussing with the captain where were World Cities, London was the first candidate he offered, as a place that had within it a world of languages and foods. It has all that and more.

~

When I was in the Texan reading room my choices were pared down. When I was typing up my notes at sea, I was there, at sea and without choices. With nearly monastic simplicity it was clear each day what I was doing: reviewing the next box of the MacNeice collection in Austin or typing up the next page of notes on the Atlantic.

Now I have been back on dry land for over a month and there are choices everywhere, particularly, and most pressingly, about the shape and direction of my next material-gathering expedition away from my desk.

Oxford was an easy hop and skip away. The whim entered my

head one evening and that is what I did the very next day. I knew the city, the places where I wanted to go and how to get there. All the usual practicalities scarcely required thinking about.

Next on the visiting list was Birmingham. Again it was a city I knew and getting there required no serious planning. I was tagging a spot of MacNeiceing on to someone else's weekend. The fixed points of where to stay and when to come and go were set. Armed with some internet sleuthing about the area where MacNeice had lived in Birmingham and a printout of how to walk from there to the address where the professor who had hired him lived, I was equipped.

I postponed for another time thinking about the shape and direction of the writing visit after Birmingham, one complicated enough to be called a 'research trip', that would require serious planning. I shut my laptop, left my desk and went north to enjoy myself with a sunnier forecast.

7

Rather on the warm side of summer

When everyone was writing with steel pen nibs it was said that three-quarters of everything that was written was written with a Birmingham nib. The nib on a quill pen had required constant sharpening. The steel pen nib did not. The steel nib made in Birmingham was then the pen nib of the egalitarian future.

It was the women who did the detailed work in the pen nib factories, while the men were downstairs rolling the steel and then firing the part-made nibs in the furnace. When the cutlery business in Sheffield took a downturn skilled craftsman came south to join the steel nib businesses that grew in Birmingham from the 1820s until the arrival of the biro in the 1950s. In Birmingham in each 10-hour day each woman was processing 18,000 nibs, each fuelling, in her way, the development of literacy and education.

All of which was news to me, when I happened upon the Pen Room Museum in the area marketed as Birmingham's Jewellery Quarter. The museum was run by volunteers, one of whom took me around the processes involved. He chided me gently for being a bit too delicate in my pulling and twisting of the handles; encouraging me to exert a firm and decisive movement as I cut a nib shape from a flat piece of steel and then curved it, before punching a hole in it and finally slitting the nib.

I fingered the small, unfinished, piece of steel, an item for revolutions in its day. The leisurely quill was made extinct by these hard-wearing, mass-produced pieces; nibs that wrote through the night blunt words of commerce or flowery words of flattery, in excitement and in boredom, nibs available to millions who had never held a quill pen.

Now writing with a nibbed fountain pen is relegated to being unusual and not quite of this world. At which point I must declare that I have not just one, but three fountain pens, all important for their associations as well as their nibs, and currently flowing with, respectively, blue, black and green ink, the latter ink colour no doubt putting me further on the fringes than would mere fountain pen possession.

The nibs of Birmingham contributed not only to the words of the world, but more locally to the words made in Birmingham, for Birmingham University grew from a college for science subjects founded with the wealth accumulated by the pen nibs of Josiah Mason.

The Pen Room Museum also had some typewriters on display. (I may have three fountain pens, but I no longer have a typewriter.)

The typewriter's carriage return did have a very satisfactory finality when the silver lever was thwacked back to its starting place. It came with the caveat that only so much frustration should be taken out on the carriage return, otherwise the return lever might exercise its right of mechanical failure at a crucial moment. The opportunity to thwack came with a crisp bell, ringing 'ting' and marking the point beyond which it was unwise to try to go. Offices were noisier then.

Pressing Enter on a keyboard is not the same, but I enjoy the freedom of changing my mind with a mere cut and paste edit and then, at the press of a button, printing out pages – though my current printer lets out a tired puff of smoke if I dare to command the printing of too many pages in one go.

Bottles of white fluid liquid paper to paint out whole words and strips of powdered white paper to type onto for the removal of a single character were things that have been and gone in my lifetime – and I do not lament their passing.

The volunteer at the museum told me how it was getting harder and harder to source ribbons for the museum's typewriters. Blotting paper can take a bit of effort to track down, but fountain pen ink is not yet a rarity.

The museum had on its door a list of the rules from one of the nib factories. Doors were locked ten minutes after the start of the morning shift and again ten minutes after the start of the afternoon shift. The afternoon shift would be extended for an extra hour in the winter if business required it. Interestingly, to a 21st century reader, it was an absolute rule that lunch was to be taken away from the workplace.

The greatest number of rules attached to how waste was to be dealt with. The starting point was that there was not to be any waste. Offcuts and other bits and pieces from each stage of the process were to be reused.

~

Birmingham did not build a cathedral when it became big enough to be granted city status. It reused a parish church. Its first bishop thought there was no need to spend money unnecessarily on buildings and as St Philip's was a relatively large church, it could serve as a cathedral too.

Having a tour around St Philip's was therefore a more digestible experience than touring other cathedrals of the realm. It had less history to recount and less architecture to trundle round. There was one main feature to focus on, the Burne-Jones windows. The windows depicted the Ascension, the Nativity, the Crucifixion and the Last Judgement, with the first three popped into a specially built extension. Burne-Jones was a local boy, born on Bennetts Hill (without an apostrophe on the road sign), just across the road from the new cathedral cum repurposed parish church.

The commissioning benefactor was a lady of decided views and she did not want to be greeted by death each time she walked in the door of her new cathedral, so the Crucifixion went into one of the side windows and she was greeted with the more uplifting prospect of Ascension in the cathedral's central window.

The church might not have been built as a cathedral but it did have a full set of 12 bells to ring out in a most cheerful fashion. The group I was with were given a tour of the bell tower, going up to see the bells hanging, not downwards as they do in Christmas cards, but, ready to ring, with the bell mouth uppermost. A selection of the bell-ringers rang an illustration of the change-ringing principles they told us about. Even to an outsider there was a certain elegance in the steady, methodical application of each peal's principles.

One bell-ringer showed a peal-ringing diagram, printed in the front of her diary. Another pulled his mobile phone from his pocket and flicked open an app which he thought would be easier for some of us to follow.

The peal boards lining the tower recorded some record-breaking peals, ringing for over ten hours and my mind wondered off to how the practicalities of that would work. For Birmingham is a practical place. Its City Council motto is 'Forward'. Not for Birmingham something fancy in Latin or some carefully composed words of flexible ambiguity, open to differences of interpretation.

Forward it says, as befits a place of railway lines and canals, a place of movement and doing.

The group I was with had been told, several times, of Birmingham having 'more canals than Venice' so later in the weekend our group regrouped to go on a canal boat ride. Just after embarkation the guide told us to look out for the turtles. We expected turtles to be a local word for some peculiarity that was specific to the waterways of Birmingham. However only a few minutes after its cue, there was indeed a turtle, sitting on a rock on the side of the canal, blending into the background, busy being a turtle, and not being shorthand for something else.

Over the course of an hour the narrow boat brought us back to where we started. The forecast sun shone and I pottered off in the unaccustomed sunshine, taking a circuitous route to a bookshop near Birmingham's New Street railway station, past yet another redevelopment of the area. Perhaps a new city centre redevelopment is like a new kitchen for each generation of town planners, a way of marking the house as being theirs and of their generation?

I retreated from the surprising heat of the afternoon and marvelled at the interior of the bookshop that once was a bank. I had forgotten about the turtles and my passing curiosity about how they got into the canals. Instead I considered my duty as aunt responsible for long words and looked for books to buy for my nieces' forthcoming outbreak of birthdays. (I had let my nephew off with a book-free birthday and had already bought him in Austin a sporting Texan Tshirt.)

I followed the bookshop's staircase downstairs, my mind still on long words. Curvaceous seemed the word for the staircase. When I took on the role of aunt responsible for long words I was remiss and did not establish how many syllables were required to qualify a word as long, but curvaceous probably counted. Not that I would want to be personally responsible for curvaceous. There was no knowing where she might go, if left unchaperoned.

The staircase certainly swept and it might, quite possibly, do it sensuously, taking curvaceous with it.

Adverbs (in metaphorical ballgowns) positioned themselves in confident announcement, proud in their rightful place once more, as the staircase ascended and descended with all the permanence that banks had in the days when the building was built. Here the adverb might rise above the emasculation meted out by sports reporters, in these days when even cricketers scoring a century play magnificent, not magnificently.

On such a staircase, the adverb might even outshine the adjective with stylish panache.

Yes, the unaccustomed sunshine had got to my grey cells.

~

After an afternoon of MacNeiceing I found a coffee shop in which to sit and take stock. The coffee shop had hard chairs assigned to desk-level working tables and soft chairs with lower-level ornamental tables. I opted for a soft chair without a working table.

A blackboard propped on top of a paperback-filled bookcase declared, 'Behind every great idea is a great cup of coffee.' With the surprising onset of summer, I opted for a fruit smoothie, not a coffee, so no great ideas for me. No sudden shafts of perceptual concepts. My stock-taking was of practicalities.

Where to go to next? Where would be my next research trip? A place for a writing visit that had a relevance to MacNeice (whether tenuous or obvious) and an interest in and of itself for me, regardless of MacNeice.

April, May and June were all now history. I had advanced into July and, despite it being the Wimbledon tennis fortnight, which is normally a byword for wet weather, summer had made a reappearance.

I had chosen to go to Austin as the first research trip of my writing year, because I wanted to go before it got brain-fryingly hot. From a climate point of view, it was Iceland that I needed to go to next, before it got darker and colder and wetter. That also suited the chronology of MacNeice who visited Iceland as he was leaving Birmingham. I was not following in the footsteps of MacNeice too literally, but it was also August when MacNeice went to Iceland, so Iceland it would be for me in August.

Iceland was where I had been as a student for two weeks of wet camping in 1986, equipped with the sagas of *The Story of Burnt Njal*, well broken-in walking boots, more than two weeks' worth of dry socks and a full set of waterproofs. That had been the first of my travels in the company of Louis MacNeice. Iceland was a place that, like Oxford and Birmingham, I would enjoy revisiting, but the practicalities of that would take some working through; they would require some serious planning and I could no longer put that off.

Or at least, once I got home to south London, I could no longer put it off.

For the immediate moment I would enjoy my fruit smoothie.

Looking around the coffee shop I realised that with so many variations of drinks all coming with their milk pre-mixed and fewer and fewer people taking extra sugar, the spoon was becoming a rarity. I could not test my theory about the depth of the bowl of a spoon being the key determinant of whether or not a spoon can be hung from a nose, or, to be more specific, whether that is the key feature as far as hanging a spoon off my nose is concerned – mine is the only nose I have ever used to test out the theory.

The job of writing a book (or two) was one I took seriously, but, even without a testing spoon to prove it, I knew that did not require me to be all serious.

'If you are happy and you know it clap your hands' goes the refrain. 'If you are happy and you can just enjoy it without either drawing attention to yourself by clapping or evaporating the happiness by dissecting it with knowing analysis' does not scan nearly so well, plus it is what my laptop underlines, in disapproving green, as only a 'fragment', one to 'consider revising'.

It is a fragment that describes the situation and dangles, avoiding any verb of consequential action.

While on the subject, my laptop also does not like 'shipping lanes' in the English Channel. It would prefer shopping lanes. It is upset by 'nibbed pens'. I think it takes them as a threat and remonstrates that any pens ought to be nibbled.

And my laptop is unhappy about being 'in a radio play'. As far as my laptop is concerned that is not a recognised place. My laptop would prefer a radio to do something, with a verb. The radio could perhaps play something.

Maybe that could be the consequential action, arising from the fragmentary moment of knowing the enjoyment of happiness. 'If you are happy and you can just enjoy it without either drawing attention to yourself by clapping or evaporating the happiness by dissecting it with knowing analysis' then listen to the radio in a coffee shop playing music to itself (and to whoever else happens to be listening).

~

I came home to the usual returning home rhythm of washing a bag of clothes and sorting post, some light displacement activity.

Part of the reason why I had been putting off getting stuck into the detailed planning of my next trip, the trip to Iceland, was that the travelling of April and May had been tiring as well as enjoyable. The onus each day had been on me to intrude on the daily lives of others. Now after two months at home I was feeling more gathered and collected, ready to do a spot more intruding.

Another part of the reason why I had put off the detailed Icelandic planning was that I now knew, from my experience in Austin and on the Atlantic, that this planning would not just be planning to go visiting a place, it would be setting myself up for the collection of the raw material of experiences on which I could then look back and type up glimpses of sunlight and poetry, the fuel for the writing months to come.

And the third part of my reason for delaying was I was enjoying myself writing, being in a place that was constant, not distracting myself with novelty.

Putting to one side the displacement activity of analysing my reasons for procrastination, I set to planning my writing visit to Iceland.

~

Iceland was in the 1980s, and is still, an expensive place. There may be more roads now than there were in the 1980s but Iceland is still a country that is larger than Wales, with a scattered population the size of Cardiff's. Which parts to visit, bearing in mind the available time and money budget? How far was I going to take the notion of 'following in MacNeice's footsteps'?

I had been camping in Iceland in 1986. I had been wet and cold and gone for a brisk walk round the campsite in waterproofs to get my blood circulating before crawling into a sleeping bag with the intention of going to sleep before the cold woke me up. Therefore I decided that this time I would move up a notch or two and book a guesthouse room, although by sharing a bathroom down the corridor from the sleeping room I would keep the price down from the open-mouthed eye-wateringly expensive to the merely eyebrow-raising surprisingly expensive.

MacNeice had ridden round a glacier with a school party. That had taken eight days. I had spent an afternoon in 1986 on a horse going through some rivers and up some inclines. I still had the notes I had made after that experience: 'My white pony had been obedient and liked water and the challenge of steep hills – but liked its own company best. At one point I charged off ahead for no particular reason. I don't know the speed of a real gallop but any faster would have been more than too fast and the trotting varied in comfort. Enjoyed the scenery rather than the pony.'

Iceland in August would be unavoidably cold and wet. There was no need to add to the discomfort by volunteering for a second experience of an Icelandic horse.

The theory is that the Icelandic horse's legs move in their diagonal pairs (so front left moving with back right and then front right moving at the same time as back left) giving a two beat trot, with points in between when no legs are on the ground, and then, says the theory, the Icelandic horse has the extra gait, the smooth (so they say) gait called the 'toelt'. One hoof at a time, first the hooves on the left side and then the hooves on the right side for a four beat toelt. I can not say whether it was two beat or a four beat discomfort I experienced in Iceland in 1986. The phrase 'my book, my rules' came again to mind. I would leave riding to MacNeice and to proper Travellers. Something else was called for, something still associated with MacNeice, but in a slightly looser way.

How about a walk instead? A two beat, left foot, right foot, human plod?

Various holidaying websites waxed lyrical about the Laugavegur trail in the southern highlands of Iceland, the majestic drama of the barren and (speak it quietly) windswept scenery. That trail is cared for by the Iceland Touring Association and as their website said, 'The difficulty of the track depends extremely on the weather conditions'. For those who, like me, no longer fancy camping in such a climate there are six mountain huts along the way. They offer, the website assured me, running cold water and showers. Continuing on the theme of cold water, I noted from the website that there were four glacial rivers to be crossed by foot, meaning no bridges, take your walking boots off and wade. Wade in this context being wading through glacial meltwater, not paddling in a stream that has had several months of summer sunshine. To quote the website again, 'Usually those crossings are harmless'. The website may have been translated from the Icelandic, but the point was still clear. There were risks attendant on glacial river crossings.

So, in summary, the website tells me hikers can expect 'beautiful views and high temperatures when the weather is good, no views at all, horizontal rain and freezing temperatures when the weather is bad'.

One of my memories from my previous visit to Iceland was of how 'to the point' Icelanders could be. The volcanic activity and glacier movements meant it was a land in constant motion, but the guide would simply say, 'If you go over there the earth's crust is very thin and you will fall through and die'. No exclamation marks. No frills. A clear and simple statement. I had come with my fellow tourists to see geology in the making. There it was. Just over there. And it could kill me, without a hierarchy of warning signs, without even pausing to check for a disclaimer of liability.

Remembering all that, I closed the tab for the Laugavegur trail website and wimped out. I decided to construct a writing visit to Iceland that involved sleeping each night in a building, with a hard roof and a soft bed, and with hot, as well as cold, running water.

As for other MacNeice places to visit, once the school summer holidays were over there was also the question of Ireland. I am so obviously English, perhaps even before I open my mouth, that I was nervous of visiting Ireland. Those nerves were compounded by MacNeice being better known in Ireland (where there was still time to teach his poetry in schools) than in England. I do not pretend to be anyone other than a layman in poetry matters and less than that when it comes to Irish history and the context for those who lived through the 20th century in Ireland. I am wary of academic territories and warier still of asking about the son of a Church of Ireland bishop in places where the labels that attach to religions have been more than usually troublesome.

Still I am reminded that the son of the Church of Ireland bishop in question was a poet, a man of words, from an island that does words and it is those words that draw me to the island, both the north and the south of it.

Where else to travel for a writing visit?

After three extremely itchy insect bites, the result of daring to sit out on an inviting patio in Austin, the idea of a trip to malarial Ghana slid down my list of places for a possible writing visit and it was pushed off the list when I found nothing in the Texan reading room from which to build a Ghanaian chapter. (MacNeice went there for the BBC on a research trip just before independence, an interesting time in Ghana's history, but not, it seemed, one MacNeice enjoyed.)

~

The late afternoon gym had only a few people scattered around the machinery. I was just into my stride, consigning to my subconscious the question of how to visit Iceland and Ireland and where else to build a writing visit, when a new employee bounced up to me. He was keen to shout through my country music soundtrack to convey his eagerness to understand my gym objectives so he could personalise a training programme just for me.

He waited expectantly for me to provide one of the answers listed on his clipboard, something about looking good on summer holiday or improving stamina for a charity challenge.

A sentence began to form in my head, but it would be unfair to lob him an answer so far from his clipboard expectations.

I am cycling, rowing and running nowhere in the gym so that I am not thinking about what I am doing next, which means that when I do think about it, I will be clearer in my thinking. How unclear is that?

Instead I closed his opening gambit with a brief, 'I am fine thanks.'

~

Having got into the habit of being hot, July 2013 remained hot. I reduced the daylight to the thin lines just permitted by the drawn slats of my wooden blinds on the window of my writing room. The puddles on my flat roof at last dried out. The grass in the back garden (too straggly to pass itself off as a lawn even at the best of times) turned brown and stopped growing.

The hot weather started to merge the days together and they in turn expanded into a sweaty coagulation of several weeks of overheated summer. I enjoyed all the more not commuting into central London dressed up in office clothes suited to a different climate. Instead the summer became one of shorts and Tshirts, items that I had not turned out of my wardrobe, despite their infrequent use, in case one day I might be in a place and a time to wear them again.

~

Now I was in the land of summer holidays, that rare place where all things seem possible and each day might, at its start, be endless. A jewel of now is suspended and then another and another, threading together a string of moments, places outside the mundane quotidian. Each of those places is reached by concentrating, by being solely and completely in that one place at that one instant of time.

Time concertinas and then stretches out into an hour of essence that lasts and lasts.

The novelty of typing at home becomes the normal. Months stretch out in front, until I bring myself back to plotting chapters against timelines, measuring up my diary against my Forth Bridge List of things to do or at least consider doing. Then it all becomes a tighter and more compact space, more the size of a city centre parking space. There is still room, but only just. There is room for a modicum of pausing, to let a chapter settle, but not scope for vast acreages of vacillation. I can permit myself some proportionate hesitation (while I decide what goes where in which book, or if it goes into a book at all), but dithering was out.

~

Well that all sounded fine, but the summer of 2013 was also a summer of Ashes cricket, five days multiplied by five locations spread through July and August where England and Australia play cricket.

I risked turning on my radio to listen, while I had my lunch, to some of the first Test match. So much for my powers of disciplined concentration. Time passed and I was still listening, long after my lunch was eaten.

The ebbs and flows of the five-day game, the traditions of it and its re-inventions, the dynamics within and between the teams, the recollections of the games I have watched and those I have listened to, all weave through the phrase 'an Ashes Summer', which I agree, on a plain English basis sounds desiccated and sombre, but words sometimes mean more than they say. Under the banner of an 'Ashes Summer' will be high drama, excitement, controversy and weather of all sorts. Not only will one team win and one team lose, there may well be, along the way, that peculiarly difficult thing to explain, the really (yes honestly) exciting draw.

By the middle of July I am making good progress with my industrious summer at the keyboard, but now, just a few clicks away, there is the BBC's *Test Match Special* website. Even if I am not listening to the ball by ball commentary of the Ashes matches on *Test Match Special* itself, there is the 'I am just looking' option of the scorecard, refreshing every few minutes on the website and augmented by the text and emails of listeners and watchers. One comes in from Geraint Jones, a name forever associated with the Ashes Summer of 2005. He has, so the website says, gone outside to check on his sheep in an effort to make England take another wicket. It works. England get another wicket. I wait for the deluge of emails to the website exhorting him to stay out with the flock so England can get the one remaining Australian wicket.

A train passenger has two hours of journey, but only three per cent of battery, left. Will England get the final wicket or will Australia get the last 20 runs before her computer goes dead? Or perhaps she might find someone on her train who has more life in their battery? An older man finds a younger man in an awkwardly outstretched position by the side of the road. The younger one is trying to get a signal to update the cricket scores. They both share a radio until lunchtime.

Lunchtime comes.

The number of balls bowled by one person before someone else has a go can be explained, since it is only fair to swop around who is throwing the ball to whom. The different ways of getting out are, in broad concept, clear. It makes sense that different people get the ball thrown at them and when everyone has messed up in one way or another, the other team see if they can do better. Even the idea that you make it a longer match by each team having two goes, two times of seeing how quickly all of them mess up, or the idea of making it a shorter match by limiting how many balls are bowled even if no batsman messes up, that too can be explained since all games need to have their rules.

But that, at the most exciting moment of a pretty exciting five days of cricket (for those of us who can say that phrase with a straight face and mean it), lunchtime comes, that can be harder to explain. Both teams stop playing for 40 minutes. Really they do. It is lunchtime.

An international, professional, 21st century sports contest stops, not for an advertising break, but for lunch and then again, in the afternoon, for tea. That is part of why I enjoy cricket. It has an in-built recognition of life outside it.

Play resumes after lunch and then all of a sudden it is indeed all over. On this occasion it is England who has won.

Sunday afternoon can now resume.

The mother who was doing her ironing in the garden because the tense nerves of Ashes cricket were getting to her (according to her son texting in to the *Test Match Special* website) can come back inside her house again. I wonder whether the lady on the train was able to hear the result before her battery finally went dead or did she have to wait, until she got to her destination, to learn of England's victory.

We all go our separate ways.

Each of us turns off the radio and closes the website, to go out and live our own lives in our own world.

For a few days that is what we do, until the first day of the second Test, when all our paths will draw closer together. For in four days' time the second Test starts at Lord's, the home of English cricket, the place where every country wants both to beat England and to do well enough for their batting or bowling (or preferably both) to be put on the honours board in the away team's dressing room.

At first we might think we will just catch up with the score at the end of the day, but then we find out the score at lunchtime and at teatime and, if we are honest, at times in between and by day three it is the weekend and the listeners to *Test Match Special* are back on trains worrying about flat batteries or trying to do their gardening, ironing or household chores while holding their breath, with fingers crossed, just for the next over and then the over after that and then the next one too. Can the newly-promoted opening batsman get a century, a hundred runs to put him on the honours board? Yes he can. Can he get two hundred? Sadly not.

Each over has six balls, six opportunities for the batsman to stroke the ball masterfully to the far corner of the ground or for the bowler to dumbfound the batsman with a ball that bounces and twists through the air, clipping the bat and being caught by the bowler before the batsman has stopped blinking.

Though that accidentally hit ball may surprise the bowler too, fumbling into the disappointment of a dropped catch.

It is all possible.

~

Like individual *Test Match Special* listeners, this book (which is the Other Book) and the Proper Book live their separate lives, each doing their own thing in their own way, but coming together from time to time when they both sit in a Texan reading room or both set off on a transatlantic voyage.

One book is not the sequel to the other; it does not follow along in its wake. Nor is one the prequel of the other; blazing a trail ahead. Perhaps this book should be content to be a metabook, if that term means a book about a book, but this book is not so content and is not fitting into that category. This book is looking out beyond the Proper Book, seeing worlds beyond the particular compass of the Proper Book. This book might be a cousin, rather than a sibling, of the Proper Book. It comes from similar roots, but while it goes to many of the same places, it also veers off to places of its own, just because it can, because it seems like fun.

My interim conclusion is that the two books are paraquels.

Yes, that is an invented word, a word to mean a book that is neither a prequel nor a sequel, but a 'going along in parallel'quel. As a description it does not quite work here, because parallel lines each go along their separate ways. Parallel lines do not come together at any point and these two books do, at many points.

I thought about walkers on a long-distance footpath. They pass and repass each other as they walk at different speeds, but I could not find a word from that image. Nor does that image quite work either. On a footpath both walkers are on the same path, whereas these two books are on different paths that sometimes merge with each other for a while and sometimes merely intersect in passing.

Perhaps this, the Other Book, is a distracted sine curve, not following the smooth, regularly repeated loops above and below the forward axis of the Proper Book. A proper sine curve would intersect the main axis at regular intervals, but the Other Book sometimes goes further away from, and sometimes stays nearer to, the main axis, and yet, for all the distractions, the one does keep coming back to the other.

A paraquel is easier to explain than a distracted sine curve, so paraquel will have to do for the moment, as this, the Other Book's description, until folks beyond these pages, having read both books, think of a better word.

~

It was the prayer ascribed to Sir Francis Drake that said, 'It is not the beginning, but the continuing of the same unto the end, until it be thoroughly finished, that yieldeth the true glory.'

Four writing months in and I have well and truly begun. This is no longer an idea for an abstract 'one day'. It is what I am doing. I am in the continuing phase. Continuing is not headline stuff. It does not have the impact of announcing, 'I am going to write a book'.

I get up and I type, day after day. After weeks, a month has past. Nothing newsworthy there.

If I am not typing, I am planning, either the next chapter or the next writing trip.

I gave myself several afternoons to book the fixed points in my August trip to Iceland and I let in to my itinerary some non-MacNeice places. Iceland has some unpronounceable parts, but it is not out of the known world in the way that a voyage on a containership was – there are advertisements for Iceland on the Northern Line platform.

Although I am not a commuter this year, I am still spending a fair amount of time waiting for Northern Line trains in my months of (sometimes metaphorical) daylight. After the typing and the planning comes the unaccustomed daylight of evenings and weekends off.

This summer I can book for BBC Proms concerts at the Royal Albert Hall and be there before the concert starts, perched on the steps of the Albert Memorial, wondering how 'Victorian' came to mean buttoned-up about emotion when such an expanse of carved marble and prominently-shone gold was put up as a memorial?

England won the second Test with a day to spare at Lord's. That has added a conversational topic to the fully-grilled barbecue of a summer we are having. Neighbouring concertgoers decided to start on their picnic, since the missing person was known for their lateness.

I have arrived for the evening's concert ahead of being early and, ungrateful for the past three weeks of deeply-heated frying, I am enjoying small hands of clouds scattered across the sky and a breeze fluttering the pages of my book.

Joggers do their rounds. Some cyclists have a schedule to keep; others wobble experimentally past me.

One of the neighbouring picnickers, pink handkerchief tucked into the breast pocket of his jacket, rang the missing one, 'On the Steps. Opposite the Hall. The Albert Memorial. It's obvious. It's big. It's like a birthday cake.'

I wondered what sort of childhood he had. My childhood birthday cakes were exemplary, but did not look like the Albert Memorial.

Inside the Royal Albert Hall I showed an Atlantic rainbow and some vistas of red containers in various weather conditions to friends. They were pictures of normality when I was on the north Atlantic; they were the views that everyone around me had. After more than two months ashore I am practised in retelling bite-sized anecdotes, but now, when I hear myself speak of my two weeks at sea on a German-flagged containership while typing up Texan research notes about a (dead) Irish poet as an opening to the book I am writing for a year, instead of being a grown-up with a job, well it all sounds (to be politely English) just a bit improbable and could, with the merest flick of a rising eyebrow, be consigned to a bucket labelled Frankly Implausible.

Let's get back to the weather. It is hot in the Royal Albert Hall. (I wonder if the pink-edged gentleman has removed his jacket.)

~

The weather for all its vagaries does give the English (and therefore me) a safe harbour amid the open shoals of potential topics of conversation. It has, however, a more important role on the fourth day of the third Test in Manchester.

It could decide the Ashes.

England were two-nil up with three matches to play. A draw in the third match would mean England would retain the Ashes because, then with only two matches to play, Australia would not be able to win the series outright and a drawn series would leave the Ashes with England, as they were the holders before the series started.

The BBC weather website referred to 'rain moving erratically', a description that makes a change from the usual pattern of bands of rain sweeping in from the west, but what would that mean for Manchester? How much playing time could be lost to rain over the final two days of the match? Would there still be enough time for Australia to win? Might just the threat of rain be enough to have an impact on the match, with anticipation of something having a greater impact than the actual happening of the something itself? What if the rain emptied out all over Birmingham and did not manage to stretch itself up to Manchester after all? Manchester, even the most ardent Mancunian, would admit, does have a tendency to rain, so two days without any rain did seem improbable, but improbable, we know, is not the same as impossible.

Sport and rain were a fitting combination for an English summer Sunday. I thought about leavening my day off from typing with some pruning, deadheading and in-ear cricket commentary. I could appear to exercise some control over my garden before I left it to its own devices while I was in Iceland. England could retain the Ashes for me, getting a draw as I gardened, before I left for possibly patchy Icelandic wi-fi.

It all sounded good in theory.

Early reports were of rain in Stockport, but which way was the wind blowing and how much rain was still in the clouds?

In south London meanwhile the sun was shining, so I left my garden to grow and took some marmalade sandwiches to The Oval, the venue at the end of the summer for the last Test match, but more often the place where the Surrey county cricket team set about beating their opposition.

The Northern Line was not being improved that Sunday so it took me to The Oval tube station where the information board warned, not of the usual delays on other underground lines, but that, 'There are no secrets which time doesn't reveal.'

Discussions about the weather forecast further north were interrupted by applause for one stump of a wicket being knocked backwards down south. It was out of kilter with its peers. It was obvious to the batsman that his time for scoring runs was past. The evidence remained for all to see.

In the stand behind me a cork was popped and sallied forth into the pale blue sky, amid cries of 'Catch it'. Sandwiches, sections of the Sunday papers and suncream were passed round. A ripple of ringpulls marked a group of friends settling in for further reminiscences of their student days. One of them handed over a phone of pictures from the night before to general agreement that the pub was better than it used to be.

Unwatched, a batsman found himself in the wrong place at the wrong time. In a county game there is no big screen to replay what happened, to show how the two batsmen mistimed their running against the fielder's throw. A runout looks slightly comical to spectators, if they are watching, but, unlike a bowled wicket, it leaves no evidence for those of us who look up, belatedly. There is just a lingering embarrassment in the batting team's dressing room.

In my ears there was a runout in Manchester too, thanks to the swift reactions of a substitute fielder. Manchester also appeared to have substitute (even non-local) weather. Has the rain been delayed? (By weekend railway improvement works?) Perhaps the rain will send bad light as its replacement to stop play?

In south London the score on the pitch ascended steadily, while behind the stands the rubbish bins were hit regularly as practising bowlers found ways past smaller sibling batsmen. Between innings at The Oval, ballgames of all sorts transferred to the outfield.

A blue denim jacket and a black leather jacket walked hand in hand, skirting carefully around the impromptu games. They matched each other's stride, both looking forward. They had decided to face together what neither was speaking about.

Above me a plane's contrails dissipated into white bands of cloud, one of which held within it a rainbow. The explanation of water droplets and refracted light does not make the multi-coloured promise that is every rainbow any less beautiful.

Bad light and rain finally arrived in Manchester; Surrey won their sunny Sunday afternoon.

~

Monday morning was not a shirt-sleeved day in south London, but Manchester took a while to live up to its rainy reputation. I typed and typed and then continued to type. When I risked looking again at the BBC's *Test Match Special* website the rain had grudgingly turned up and with it, later on in the afternoon, came the drawn Test match that retained the Ashes in England.

The summer of Ashes uncertainty was over.

For me Austin, Charlotte and Wilmington were also in the known past and I was readying myself to visit 1930s Iceland. Once more I made a projection of my travelling writer self as I packed my suitcase. Once more I made a supper of the perishables left in my fridge.

Map showing places visited in Iceland
(spelling of names anglicised)

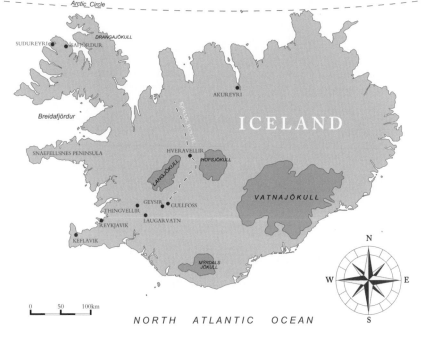

8

Rainbows at the end of the season

The Keflavik airport terminal I remembered from my first visit to Iceland in 1986 was a strictly functional place, where civilian planes were allowed to land on what was essentially an American air force base.

Times changed. The Americans left and the NATO base closed in 2006. Icelandair positioned itself as a carrier linking Europe and North America. (Indeed Iceland's place between two worlds, not just two continents, was put to use, when Presidents Reagan and Gorbachev met there, also in 1986, their meeting marking, some would say, the beginning of the end of the cold war.)

Modern Keflavik's 'new' terminal opened in 1987 and it now has all the mod cons of an architect-designed commercial airport, including shopping on the way to and from the flight and modern art littered about.

There is, for example, a pile of rocks in front of the terminal building, on top of which is a large shiny metallic egg, perched slightly precariously. The egg is big enough to belong to some, as yet undiscovered, dinosaur and is beginning to crack. A savage hook, the tip of a serious claw protrudes from the egg. Apparently the protrusion is the start of a jet's wing. (Remind me not to fly on whichever plane the artist was looking at when he was working on this sculpture.)

On the airport's perimeter there is another sculpture, more to my taste, also by an Icelandic artist. It is a slightly curved tower made of stainless steel and with stained red, yellow, green and blue glass inserted here and there, waiting to reflect the sunlight that will come. It is the start of a rainbow, a recognition that there will be both rain and sun, the only question being as to the proportions.

If I had been taking my MacNeiceing to a higher level of seriousness I would have gone from Keflavik to meet a guide and a horse prior to spending a week riding round the nearest sizeable glacier, camping each night. Having decided that I was neither camping nor riding, but writing, I went instead into the eaves of a Reykjavik guesthouse that was within walking distance of both the bus station and the domestic airport as well as the centre of the city and there enjoyed sleeping inside a building on a wet and windy night.

Equipped with a well-laid out tourist map in my bag I set off the next morning. Twenty paces down the road, I was asked for directions to the swimming pool, so with the aid of my map we plotted a route for my questioner and I wondered what was written on my forehead that made me look as if I would know, within hours of arriving in a city, the answer to directions? Or was it a question of height? I was short enough to be interrupted?

In Reykjavik's old harbour the displays of the maritime museum reflected the impact of the herring coming or not coming, the harvests being good or not good, the world of boom and its sudden inexplicable absence, in such a way that the collapse of the Icelandic banks and the country's resultant parlous financial state in 2008 seemed just another manifestation of the good times abruptly ending at the point when people thought this time was different, this time the boom was not a bubble.

In the boom times for herring from 1902 to 1930 the annual catch increased five times, doubling the number of fisherman at sea and tripling the number of people working onshore in fish processing, but there was emigration too. Volcanic eruptions, earthquakes and hard winters all drove 20,000 to emigrate to north America between 1870 and 1914.

The maritime museum also made clear some of the costs of the fishing booms. Between 1900 and 1925 there was an average of 70 lives lost at sea each year. Another display had a map showing where the 152 ships and 400 lives were lost around the coast of Iceland from 1928 to 1937. (Iceland's population in 1936 was about 110,000, of which 30,000 lived in Reykjavik.) It was estimated that about 10,000 were on the streets of Reykjavik for the first 'Seaman's Day', 6 June 1938. The date of 6 June was chosen because the winter fishing season ended on 11 May. The idea was to set aside a day to remember those who had died at sea in the past year and raise money for the support of their families. By 6 June those who had not come home in May, were not coming home.

Away from the harbour, the National Museum of Iceland was just what I was looking for, enabling me to learn more about

Iceland generally and also about how it would have looked in 1936 to British tourists, such as MacNeice and Auden. This museum set out the history and geology of the area in a way that flowed through the displays, allowing each visitor to pace themselves. There were some buttons to press and headsets to listen to, but the chosen technology seemed more of a tool to share knowledge than the gimmicks so often indulged in by museums eager to display their relevant modernity. Details were picked out as an illustration of a wider theme.

The museum took me from early settlers (the younger sons without farmsteads or the disgruntled losers in the restructuring of Celtic or Scandinavian kingdoms) past trading with the English, the Dutch and the German Hanseatic League, before colliding with the grimness of the 18th century. No wonder the then ruling Danes thought about evacuating the remnants of the population from Iceland: smallpox, famine and earthquake, plus volcanic eruptions that darkened the sun as far away as Japan and may have contributed to the French revolution, as the falling ash affected the harvest.

It was not until 1944 that Iceland became once more an independent country with a flag that has the asymmetrical cross of Scandinavian countries with, the blurb assured me, colours of sky blue, fire red and snow white. Iceland (like Norway) is not in the EU, but overlaps with it in some matters of trade by being in the European Economic Area.

Indeed it seems that the similarities of geography and history lend Iceland to partnering with Norway. Fjords and fishermen give them more in common with each other (some 600 miles apart) than with Denmark, the flatter pastoral place nearly 1,200 miles from Iceland that ruled them both.

The National Museum had a display of photographs taken in the 1860s by Sigfus Eymundsen. There were worthies of the time suitably posed: bookshelf behind and black and white tiles underfoot. In fact every single worthy had bookshelves behind and black and white tiles below. The bookshelves behind were painted onto a piece of cloth hung to achieve the desired effect and the black and white tiles were on a sheet rolled out for each portrait. (Sometimes the assistant did not get it quite right and the bottom of the portrait included rough earth.) There were also pictures of ice in the harbour at Isafjordur in August 1866. (I too would be visiting Isafjordur in August, but planned to leave before the end of August, when snowstorms were forecast.)

I moved on to sample the Museum of Photography, expecting to see more dramatic landscapes and historic worthies. Instead I came into a roomful of untroubled blue skies and wide and smooth roads, as the display of the moment was a portfolio of photographs taken of Harley-Davidson motorcycles in and around Daytona Beach in Florida with their, usually bearded, owners, looking like people with whom I might not choose to share a table in a coffee shop. Unusually there was no admission fee for that museum, so although I did not see what I was expecting there, I did not pay to experience that incongruity.

It was still raining when I came out from that unexpected burst of very foreign sunshine.

The National Gallery of Iceland was not quite what I was expecting either: a display of bits and pieces rather than a narrative whole, but just when I was consigning myself to the box marked, 'Verbal not visual', I came across a series of five wooden boxes, about the size of shoeboxes. The lid to the top of each box was open and then one (or sometimes two) of the side flaps were also unclipped and opened. Inside each box was a different layout of houses and hills, looking like an extract from a model railway layout or the outskirts of an architect's model. 'Katrin Sigurdardottir', the label said. Representing Iceland in the Venice Biennale of 2013 and living and working in New York, said some blurb I later found. That blurb then veered off to talk about perceptual experience and I changed the label on my own box to say, 'Not verbal about visual'. I knew the meaning of each individual word in the blurb, but when put together the whole was an incomprehensible sum of the parts.

There was a moment as I left the National Gallery of Iceland when I did consider taking off one of my layers of clothing. There was enough sun for shadows to be patterning the street.

I saw a family group of three ducks, out on the Tjorin, translated as pond but fully deserving of the name lake. I wondered about calling the duck family 'Goldeneye'? But then Iceland is where American and European birds meet and my bird book told me Barrow's goldeneye came over from the US. Were these well-built goldeneyes (assuming that to be their proper plural) or normal-sized American Barrow's goldeneyes (which looks difficult to have correctly in the plural), larger than European goldeneyes and, my bird book says, heavier-built than them?

A jet of water spouted as an ornamental fountain for the city lake (or pond or just plain Tjorin) and was blown in several directions at once, forming a mist veil. The moment for taking off a fleece layer passed as the clouds rolled back.

Over the course of the next few days I tried various different coffee places in Reykjavik. The intermittent rain acted as music does for a game of musical chairs with tourists. When the rain stopped we all went out and when it was raining the impression was of slightly too few chairs for the number of brightly-coloured waterproofs in search of them.

The centre of Reykjavik had its fair share of heavy granite building blocks and worthies standing around in frock-coats on pedestals. There was an outbreak of late 20th century trophy buildings too, including the Harpa concert hall, full of glass and slightly disconcerting angles, which was well-endowed with sitting places for sheltering tourists and with sofas, comfortable for those who had longer thigh bones than mine.

Reykjavik's domestic streets were also the streets with commercial buildings in, so stuccoed concrete and painted corrugated iron were never far away. Children's scooters and rubber boots were tangled in the porch between outer and inner door. Prams too were often outside the house, not, it seemed, because there was no room inside, but because fresh air was considered a good thing for sleeping babies. It was also the case that the prams were substantial, the type that really deserved the full title of 'Perambulator' with four wheels supporting a well-sprung horizontal base into which slotted a hooded carry-cot, not a quick release padded bucket that strapped into a car seat.

Pottering around Reykjavik I came across a pair of houses. Not very strange to see semi-detached houses, other than that, on closer examination, this pair appeared to house the British and the German embassies.

Another street had a detached house demarcated by chest-high concrete blocks, painted white and planted with pansies: the US embassy.

Another observation from my potterings in and out of places in Reykjavik was that the automatic sliding doors were set to open only in that moment just before my nose smudged the glass. Perhaps I was still walking around at the pace of a London commuter, not that of an average tourist? Or perhaps, although heating buildings was cheap thanks to the geothermal power, they did not want to let out any of that hot air on account of passersby who were not coming in?

Even where there was a conventional door that I could open at the very moment when I was ready to go through it, there was often an automatic closer attached to it, so it came as no surprise to see a stone in the Settlement Exhibition that archaeologists thought was a weight that had been used to close a door in 871, when the first people came to settle in Iceland.

The Settlement Exhibition was in a dimly-lit basement, because that was where stones (from a wall in the first place of human settlement in Iceland) were discovered when digging foundations for yet another Reykjavik hotel in 2001. Icelandic and English descriptions labelled what had been found and what could be deduced from that. (The contents of a rubbish heap do sound more scholarly and worthy of academic study when labelled as being the contents of a midden.) The conclusion at the time of the exhibition's labelling appeared to be that archaeology does not disagree with the *Book of Icelanders*. That was a book thought to have been written down in 1130 and previously that book was not thought to be accurate in a historian's sense, yet it tracked the first settlement back to a time that we might call 871.

The exhibition included a physical scale model reproduction of the long hall of the Vikings, as it would have been in the tenth century, and a computer screen model that was touch-sensitive and came up with fuller information in English and Icelandic if stroked in a certain way.

The main feature of the exhibition was, as it should be, the stones themselves. As I walked around the stones, the dimly-lit basement changed to being a place where people lived; all because of the projection of a very realistic flame, dancing in the hearth (with the aid of a plastic screen) in the middle of the stones that built the long hall. With the aid of that flame I could hear sagas being declaimed through the babble of a revelling feast. Without the flame it was a mildly interesting exhibition in a time of rain.

Despite enjoying the enlivening effect of the flames at the Settlement Exhibition and all the comprehensive detail of the National Museum of Iceland, it was the specific detail of the Culture House, the museum of manuscripts, that made that my favourite exhibition in Reykjavik. The labelling there took me back to the time before the steel pen nibs of Birmingham and described the preparing of skins, the making of the parchment on which scribes laboured with their quill pens.

One in ten Icelanders writes a book, says an oft-repeated factoid, though to balance that enthusiasm the Culture House quoted an eighth century scribe gloomily recording that his work, 'dulls the eyes, constricts the kidneys and torments all the joints'. I relished the fact that peering at those manuscripts in the soft-lighting to preserve them, I traversed centuries, at a glance going back to the 12th century writing down of tenth century stories. These are not like electronic documents whinging that they are in an incompatible file format and that the programme to open them can not be located. Even without knowledge of Icelandic, I can enjoy the illuminated initial capital letters, some with faces drawn within them, others with caricatures or gargoyles growing out from them.

The pen the scribes used was usually a quill taken from one of the larger birds: swans, geese or crows. The feather was then sharpened with all the skill that the steel nibs of Birmingham made redundant. Apparently the left wing's feathers were thought to be easier to use. (I heard elsewhere that the Bank of England continued to use quills into the early 20th century.) Turning animal skin into parchment for writing required the removal of the animal's hair. The blurb mentioned lime solutions and much scraping and stretching and re-scraping and re-stretching. It also referred obliquely to the use of urine in some places.

Njal's Saga was the saga of which there were the most manuscript copies extant and so that is thought to have been the most popular. In that story one of the lead characters, Gunnar, stayed on in Iceland after his sentence of exile had been pronounced, demonstrating a love of his country despite his enemies and providing a heroic figure of patriotism when one was needed in the 19th century as Iceland began to build itself towards the independence from Denmark that came in 1944.

Not being Icelandic however I read that section as an almost comic episode: man falls off horse and while lying on the ground slightly dazed, he realises what a wonderful country he lives in and decides not to leave it, despite the terms of his agreed sentence of exile.

The lawyer in me did not approve of Gunnar reneging on his promise to leave Iceland for three years. At the point when everything was packed and his close comrade was also ready to embark and discharge the terms of his promise, Gunnar rode off over the horizon, leaving his friend to go into exile alone. Not on really.

~

I was spending time in Reykjavik before meeting up with a party of yoga students. I was not joining them to ride around a glacier as MacNeice and Auden had with the party of schoolboys they met up with, but to travel by bus around the peninsula of Snaefellsnes. When the yoga students were having a two-hour yoga session each morning, I would have my own writing time carved out from the planned schedule.

Is the collective noun for a group of yoga students a Mat? (Let's assume it is and then I can write about the group of yoga students as a collective, the Mat, and thereby honour my promise that I would not be writing about any one individual.)

I went with the Mat to The Blue Lagoon. It was better to go to The Blue Lagoon while I did not yet know the individuals that made up the Mat. Being very English I think we all found the nude showering protocol before dressing to enter the pools, understandable in the absence of chlorination of the pools, but disconcerting, and better done with strangers than with people you knew, however slightly.

The Blue Lagoon is on the way to and from Keflavik airport and had not been invented as a tourist destination when I first passed that way in 1986. Someone from another part of Iceland described it as 'runoff from the power station', which it is. Hot water coming out of the ground is harnessed in several ways, one of which is to fuel the nearby geothermal power station and once that is done the runoff goes into an irregularly-shaped pool, branded a Lagoon, to increase international tourists' spending.

I found myself explaining, mostly in sign language, how to use the electronic wristbands that locked the clothes lockers (and that 'know' if you have bought a drink from the poolside bar) to a Japanese fellow tourist and then to her friend (all while I was not fully dressed myself).

In the main pool itself there were places where bathers from around the world congregated to slop out gloop with ladles and smear it over their faces, making themselves look like the advertisements for the Blue Lagoon I had seen while waiting on the Northern Line platform. The gloop and the silica suspended in the milky-blue water is said to do all sorts of things to the skin. The silica coated my hair (which can already, when it so chooses, stand upright, without the aid of additional substances). The silica scoured under my fingernails. The gloop and silica set me thinking, as I bobbed around in the soothingly warm water, about the impressive efficiency of the processing of the naturally-heated water and the time-constrained bathers. The changing rooms were built for taking clothes off; if I wanted to sit down I could do that elsewhere, perhaps in the cafe, while spending money. I can admire an efficient machine, but such admiration is not necessarily relaxing.

The next morning, while the Mat was yogaing, I took myself out into the early morning sunshine, across the hotel's golf course. (Apparently Iceland has in 2013 got one golf course for every 4,000 or so Icelanders. This rash of pock-marking sand bunkers was another change since 1986. I preferred the statistic of Iceland having the highest number of Nobel prize-winners per head, with Halldor Laxness having won the Nobel prize for Literature in 1955, long before he died in 1998.) In front of me was a little finger of a fjord inlet, behind that confident mountains, sharply-focused against a blue sky that, even that early, was ranging through the spectrum from pale to deep blue. Birds that I would not hazard to name from the 'little brown job' section of my bird book called and answered each other from low-level bushes. Some small white and purple meadow flowers waved in the breeze at my feet, because, before I get too lyrical, there was still a noticeable breeze of the fresh, unpolluted air of Iceland. (I use the term breeze, so that I can refer to wind when there was more of it later in the day.)

Being a land-based mammal, this (not slopping around in silica-laden bathing water) was a place for me to relax, walking through grassland, at the edge of a new day, with fresh light casting the shadows that belong to that time.

Staying in a hotel with a golf course was not my usual habitat, but it did allow me to graze the internet over breakfast to check on the state of the third day of the fourth Test and see that England had made a recovery from what had seemed like a lost cause in the latest Ashes cricket match. As ever the player that some commentators insist on calling 'hugely talented' had given his wicket away cheaply and it was the less acclaimed Ian Bell that had scored a century for England.

As we made our way along the Snaefellsnes peninsula (and here I have to admit I have wimped out of finding the correct combination of key taps and so have 'anglicised' the spellings of the Icelandic names) the majority of the Mat opted for another hot springs-fed swimming pool. This pool was in term-time the pool of the school next door and it was a world away from the large-scale processing of The Blue Lagoon.

More 'little brown job' birds bounced from grass to fence and then off and away beyond the edge of the school playground. A paler wagtail than the pied wagtail of south London strutted his stuff on the gravel. I confidently called him a white wagtail – and he did not disagree.

Later that day three birds hurried self-importantly across our path as we made our way to the beach of black rocks, beyond the small and picturesque black wooden church at Budir on the Snaefellsnes peninsula. The Mat's tour bus driver confirmed them to be ptarmigan. Perched on the grassed bank above the beach I managed to pick out the call of the oystercatchers on my own.

The purple-tinged grass was indeed whispering, reminding the Mat and me of how lucky we all were to have such a fine day. We walked the rocky path from Arnarstapi (making the best of its fame as the starting point for H G Wells when, purely in his imagination, he took his readers to the centre of the world) to Hellnar (another hotel with finer dining than the dried fish of MacNeice's 1936 expedition round a glacier), seeing the path in picture-postcard conditions. The rock formations along the walk's route were striking, but without a person to helicopter onto a convenient rock, it was difficult to give an idea of scale when taking photographs of them.

It was said that whales were sometimes seen in the bay just beyond the hotel at Hellnar, but I found a sofa in the hotel's lobby with a good wi-fi signal and a whale could have waved a tail fin and posed to give scale to a photograph of the bay and I would not have noticed. The final stages of the fourth day of the fourth Test had been waiting for me to join them.

Stuart Broad had been taking wickets while I had been admiring rock formations and although I had only got into my seat in time for the last two overs of the day's scheduled play, England had come close enough to a winning result by then that the rule about playing on beyond the scheduled close of play was invoked.

The ebb and flow that is a proper Test match had come to this: could the final wicket be taken by England, thereby winning (not just retaining) the Ashes before the Mat gathered for dinner?

I waited for the *Test Match Special* website to refresh. The breeze had strengthened to a noticeable wind. A white wagtail on the decking outside the window was not bouncing with normal wagtail ebullience, but had its head tucked into its neck.

One more ball was all that was needed to win the Ashes properly. None of this retaining what you have not lost, but a proper win with just one ball, but it had to be the right ball, going to the right place.

The website refreshed with news that the wicket-keeper had missed a run out. He had the chance to get the ball to where the batsman should have been, before the batsman was. The wicket-keeper failed.

The teeth-gnashing of the first few days of the fourth Test match in Durham was now nail-biting instead. Just one ball. Just one more ball, but a ball that takes a wicket.

The website refreshed once more. England had won the Ashes again. That sentence was unimaginable for so many years.

Not only did England win, they did it with a few minutes to spare before dinner was served.

The hotel at Hellnar prided itself on sustainability and instead of chocolates there was placed a small laminated card on my pillow. Card number 32 in their series said, 'I value every moment of my life'.

~

The next day normal service had been restored. The mountains were removed by cloud. Long before I got up the rain was tapping on the window. A day for museums as the brightness came and went and then cheered up again, as if on an undecided dimmer switch.

A day for rainbows. There was sun before and after the rain that itself preceded and succeeded the sun.

On the mud of a river's estuary a coterie of redshanks, given away by their eponymous red legs, gathered and then took off in contagious alarm.

Arctic terns swooped on their targets, getting straight to their point, angular and uncompromising.

Freed from checking opening times and directions for myself I had the luxury of going along wherever the Mat's tour bus went. By Bjarnarhofn the rain had softened from the vehemence that had sent us into a supermarket's cafe for lunch. The rain was now at the dampening end of the 'still really raining' spectrum. Here there was a small church of painted wood on a slate foundation, built on top of a place that had been the site of a church since Iceland converted to Christianity in 1000.

The Althing (the annual assembly of the chiefs since 930 and therefore acclaimed as the first Parliament) had met as usual in 1000 and decided someone else should decide what to do about Christianity. The Althing gave that question to a pagan. He took himself off for a day and spent that day under his cloak thinking. His conclusion was that two religions in one place was not a good idea, so, to the surprise of those who had expected a different answer, his view was all should become Christian, at least in public.

The Mat walked from the tour bus down to the locked church and, while waiting for the key-holder to come, one by one we tried out each wall of the church, thinking that one wall, surely, must be in the lee of the wind.

The key-holder came to the church, letting us all in to shelter from the wind and bringing with him tales of things seen and unseen, the stories behind what we could see. The chalice was said to give off a heat and the eyes of the Jesus-figure on the altar-piece were said to follow the viewer.

In the Icelandic saga of Njal there were those who could see things before they happened. (Accurate prediction may come from seeing clearly the way things are and not getting distracted by how things are not.) The wisdom shown by characters in the sagas and legends may be that rooted in insights drawn from the knowledge of how people are or there may be something else. On the Snaefellsnes peninsula there is said to be an energy and force from the mountains themselves.

For all the attraction of replicable experiments, there are, in my opinion, more ways of knowing than purely that based on historic evidence.

And my basis for saying that? Why historic evidence of course!

My father was a practical man, from whom 'Don't be silly' was a strong admonishment, yet he could find water by dowsing with two pieces of bent wire. He used the tool of a camera to take photographs and the tool of dowsing rods to find underground streams. Photography could be explained. Dowsing could not yet be explained, but that did not stop it working for him.

~

No, as yet unexplained, dowsing skill was required to find the water on the Mat's boat trip from the town of Stykkisholmur on the Snaefellsnes peninsula, around Breidafjordur, looking at the rock formations of some of the approximately 3,000 islands sprinkled across that fjord and watching those birds that had not yet left.

Rain was in the atmosphere, not forming into a time-specific event, but just being there, sharing the sky with a light that brightened and darkened and brightened again, shading from lightly-washed off-white to glowering black, through a spectrum of greys.

The main event of the morning was watching puffins. They build a burrow two metres long, with one room at the end for the nest and another for 'waste', their midden. Puffins do not look as if they are built for digging, so I was not surprised to hear it can take two years to dig the nest, unless a couple take over a disused one. They also do not really look built for flying, their stubby wings seemed awkward in clumsy flight. Floating around at sea, in apparent tubby contentment, with their brightly-coloured beak making them look as if they are cheerful, is what they seem to be best suited for.

We saw kittiwakes close up, the young looking better-dressed than their parents, and fulmars did several fly-pasts for us. We watched cormorants hanging their wings out to dry, in a time of less dampness than was to come. There was no doubt all of them needed to speak to their PR agencies. No cuddly cormorants for sale as soft toys in the local shops, no kittiwakes on a key-ring and fulmars too did not feature as a retail opportunity. The market in bird-related souvenirs had been completely cornered by the puffins.

The morning's boat ride also added to our collection of basalt column pictures. Some were in horizontal pancake layers, one set were being thrust out at differing angles on different parts of the island, a veritable exhibition of geological formations. Most of the basalt came in the straight up and down, vertical variety of columns. The Mat had already done towering basalt columns earlier in the week but those had been set against a pure blue sky when we stopped for a walk along the foot of the cliffs at Gerduberg, on entering the Snaefellsnes peninsula. Now we had some harsher, rainswept columns.

Basalt columns in any setting did tend to superlatives, being monumental displays of force, whether those are the scientific forces of the earth's energy at the columns' creation or the legendary forces wrought by emotional gods venting their frustrations.

The boat ride concluded with the nautical equivalent (to me) of watching paint dry – namely watching water rush out at 18 knots between two neighbouring islands at high tide. Most of the boat's passengers were in the saloon below. The islands, whether green and low-lying or brown and steeply rocky, had begun to merge into each other, a picture of a harsh life in the days when the islands were lived on year round. We saw some of the summer houses built now for holidaying town-dwellers and even that seemed no picnic.

~

Stykkisholmur itself had a white church on the hill opposite the Mat's hotel. It was a church unlike the simple red and white or plain green and white churches that I had been trying to photograph on my journeying around Iceland. This was determinedly modern in its white concrete, a mixture of curves and spikes. The church had been consecrated in 1980, after its architect had died. It was said to have been designed by a dentist, though I was not sure whether that was a joke for gullible tourists to fall for or another example of Icelanders covering a range of jobs in their careers, like the first woman President of Iceland having been, not a politician, but a tour guide and theatre director with several degrees, before she was elected to the presidency in 1980.

Down in the town were many houses built in Stykkisholmur's times of prosperity. The Norwegian House was built in 1832 with timber that the first owner shipped over in his own ship, the timber lengths ready-sawn in Norway. At a time when turf houses were usual, to build a two-storey house was a first, even perhaps an indication of the oddity of Arni Thorlacius, the trader who built it and lived here.

Walking around his home (now a museum) the contrast with the small museum of turf houses I had visited the day before was marked. Here the rooms were lit by windows, the doors were tall enough to walk through easily, and each room could have a purpose different from its neighbour as there were enough of them. Even walking up stairs would have been a novelty for the merchants and farmers who would have visited Arni Thorlacius here.

Arni Thorlacius' most unusual habit (and the one for which he has now achieved some fame) was that of keeping for nearly 50 years very detailed weather observations on his customised recording sheets.

The weather also featured on the other side of the town where what had been the library was now an art installation, The Library of Water, with 24 glass columns each containing water from a different glacier in Iceland, and various weather words on the floor, some in English and some in Icelandic. There was no doubt an artistic reason why the one word that the artist (Roni Horn) chose to put on the olive green Tshirts for sale was 'Clammy'. Not being artistic I can not imagine fronting up to the world with the word 'Clammy'. Some of the phrases from the BBC's *Shipping Forecast* would perhaps be more practical to use on souvenirs: a beach towel saying 'showers later' or a satchel saying 'moderate becoming good'?

As Roni Horn says, in her blurb for the installation, the weather is strongly present in everyday life in Iceland. My trousers flapped determinedly in a bid for freedom as I walked back to the hotel.

Although the majority of the population now live in urban areas Iceland is a place of the outdoors. That was illustrated as I walked through a covered shopping centre. Having bought some supplies at the supermarket, I passed a shop selling hard-wearing clothes for the outdoors and just inside the entrance was a display of shoes, ranged in size from smaller to larger. The shopper made their selection and took their chosen shoes to the central counter to pay. The reason why the display had stopped me in my tracks was that the shoes were horseshoes. Bread and apples, yes; pair of horseshoes, no, they were not on my shopping list, but then I was resolutely not riding, but travelling by bus.

By the time the Mat's bus had got back to Reykjavik we could all recognise a basalt column when we saw it. There was the Catholic church with attendant architectural versions of basalt columns. Basalt columns again as the motif flanked the main Lutheran church. Those columns looked over the capital from behind the bronze statue of Leif Erikson. He was the first European by some accounts to set foot on north American soil, though the plaudits for performing that role are more commonly given to Christopher Columbus.

Basalt columns came into play in the sculpture of Einar Jonsson whose museum is nearby Leif's statue. One sculpture had a female head on a sphinx's body with basalt columns for wings and various bodies strewn under her, including, I think, a body of Death, though the label said *Mother Nature*. Another sculpture had two skinny men leaning, exhausted, against a horse, itself propped up by some cut-down basalt columns: nothing glamorous about this *Indebtedness*. There seemed to my eyes to be a mismatch in Einar Jonsson's sculptures between the details (being intricate) and the scale of the works themselves (being imposing and suitable for large public spaces).

The sculptures of Asmundur Sveinsson (who was also working in Iceland in the 1930s) were more rounded and when I came across them in my Icelandic travels they seemed more fitted to the scale of their place. There was a *Water-Carrier* in the centre of Reykjavik, whose two pails of water weighed down a woman in the manner of someone struggling with two heavy bags of shopping, and in the north-west of Iceland, in a small park in Isafjordur I came across a sculpture that was suffused with sadness, a windswept woman, trying to protect the child left to her. Not a basalt column in sight there.

When I went up to the far north to Akureyri, there they were again, the representations of basalt columns. There was a complete circumference of them surrounding the Hof, the building that housed the concert spaces for the city as well as the tourist information office. Basalt columnar representations did flanking duty again for the Akureyri cathedral on its hillside perch. That cathedral also had in its main window some of the glass from Coventry's original medieval cathedral. The route of the glass (from being tucked away in a farm for safe-keeping during the second world war to being for sale in a London antiques shop) was not described on the display just inside the cathedral's door. That display showed the former, slightly dumpy parish church of 1930 being transformed in the early 1940s into its new role of being a landmark piece of architecture.

More actual basalt columns were to be seen when, on a bus trip out from Akureyri, I saw Godafoss, the waterfall where the pagan who had ruled in favour of Christianity, threw his pagan idols away, on his return home from that year's Althing.

I did the full trio of principal Icelandic waterfalls adding Dettifoss, said to be the most powerful waterfall in Europe, while I was in the north, and in the south, Gullfoss, the curved waterfall of a two-stage drop that the tour buses tie in with the geysirs at Geysir and the site of the Althing at Thingvellir. Gullfoss and Geysir had more signage than when I passed that way in 1986 but the boardwalks and roping off were not intrusive and the noticeboards were gently informative. Both were still places that for all their fame, and even now some packaging for tourists, showed the power of the elemental forces, the ice, water and fire that made Iceland.

As in 1986 I concluded that the better pictures of Gullfoss were those from higher up, where I could get some sense of the size of the waterfall and the better pictures at Geysir were the ones my eye saw, with the plume of water nicely framed, since the camera only got steam and subsiding water. The Great Geysir that gave its name to the place (and even the phenomenon of boiling spurts of water) had had so much thrown into it over the years that it no longer performed at all. That job was now undertaken by Strokkur, spouting every six minutes.

My impression of Thingvellir in 1986 was not helped by the rain. 'Breakfast under brollies in gloom' said my holiday diary then, adding that I found it hard to populate a marshy river valley with Icelandic elders. The weather was better in 2013 and I recognised the church nestled amid the stream-threaded valley of Thingvellir, a valley well-suited for large gatherings. However the recently-installed boardwalk and visitors' centre (with fee-charging toilets) had made a new place and one that I still found difficult to populate with the shades of its famous past.

Here, we were told, the Eurasian and American plates are moving apart at 7mm a year, so that, and some severe earthquakes at the turn of the new century, helped me justify why I did not recognise in that place the rubbled rift valley I had slithered through in pouring rain in 1986.

By the time I got back to Reykjavik in 1986 I was extolling in my diary the virtues of a hot shower and enjoying the opportunity of siting down on a chair at a table while watching a pink-clouded sunset. This time, as my tour with the Mat came to its end, the sun was again shining.

Saturday translates literally in Icelandic as 'washday', but I had done my chores and had sufficient supplies of dry socks so I took instead pen, paper and sandwiches over to Videy, an island a brief ferry ride out into the bay in front of Reykjavik.

On our small ferry families, complete with full-scale

perambulators, were clambering aboard with supplies, to visit their favourite picnic spot. Two small girls looked as if they were demonstrating just how very, very good they had been so that they did get taken horse-riding after lunch.

It was now mid-August, which was halfway through the nine months of the writing part of my writing year, so a good day to do nothing very much in particular, just enjoy the day, screen-free and obligation-free, without my Forth Bridge List in sight.

I had sufficiently got the hang of the idea of Just Being that I did not even take the free map of Videy that was being given away on the ferry. That map marked out all the possible landmarks that a brisk walker could tick off in a sharp couple of hours. The blue sky of that Saturday was not one for end to end walking, though I did look into the small church, next to the restaurant doing good business on its sunny tables. The blurb in the church described how the pews for the women on one side of the church were seven centimetres lower than those for the men on the other, but the feature in the church most striking to me was that the pulpit was above the altar, quite literally elevating words above all else.

A blonde-haired girl of about six came into the church and told me something. What sort of a grown-up was I? I had no idea what she had told me. I gestured emptily that I did not understand Icelandic.

Outside I found a place out of the wind to watch the red-hulled containership of the Royal Arctic Line set off for Greenland. Out in the bay too were yachts with their spinnakers full of wind. A solitary gannet came in from the sea and frightened up a flock of starlings. Behind me the whole spine of Mt Esja was visible, not just to me, but to all of Reykjavik. There was a single, merely decorative, cloud casting a hand-shaped shadow on its slopes. It was an afternoon to be bottled, before the summer season faded into memories.

In 1986 going to Iceland was not unheard of, but it was unusual. By 2005 there were 383,000 reported tourists in the year – more people came to visit the country than lived in the country as residents. Now as the 2013 tourist season drew to a close Iceland was expecting to have seen as visitors more than twice the number of its own population, with an expected 727,000 visitors. Even in the middle of the nowhere that was Hveravellir, a camping place with hot springs in the heart of the interior, reached (if on a bus) only after several hours of rough gravel track across the Kjolur plain to the east of Langjokull glacier, 30,000 people came. That is 30,000 people visiting during the two (or maybe three) months in which the road there is open.

How to manage the tourists who come to see that which risks becoming invisible under the weight of tourists who come to see it? That is a challenge for all places where tourists are a substantial income stream.

As I moved away from the area around Reykjavik the challenge was less visible. The pseudocraters of Skutustadir or the dark lava formations of Dimmuborgir are very much on the tourist trail, but that trail is less intensely travelled than the heavily-marketed 'Golden Circle' of Gullfoss, Geysir and Thingvellir in the south. Displaying recognisable regional one-upmanship, the brochure about those northern sights within easy reach of Akureyri did refer to them as being part of the 'Diamond Circle'.

When the Mat took itself home to a place where the hot water does not smell, my next chapter was a bus journey north, through the stony interior, to Akureyri and its sights.

9

More basalt columns

The brochure for the scheduled longer-distance bus journeys referred to their routes as giving their passengers a 'full unpainted experience', which did seem a suitable phrase as I looked out of the window of the bus. I was heading towards the Kjolur plain into what was, at that moment, the bleak monotone grey of the rain-lashed interior.

Unlike the bus we travelled on in 1986, the bus of 2013 on the Kjolur route through the interior was hardened to the task. This time I did not get multiple opportunities to examine the roadside rocks as we did not have any punctures, but we did still have one unscheduled opportunity to stretch our legs and look around at the emptiness, when the driver stopped to change into overalls and out of sandals before he swept up the glass that lined the floor after one of the side windows shattered. It was only the inner glass that broke when a stone hit the outer glass. The safety glass passed its test as chunks of it slipped down the inside of the outer window, with slow-motion inevitability, collecting on the floor. No splinters of glass shredded the air; just an orderly descent of clear, mosaic-tile shapes.

The driver told us that we had not even got to the Kjolur

yet, with the implication being that things would be rougher there. The Kjolur was a place that had a reputation for being where things happened, things that were not entirely explicable.

It did not look that different on the map, the point where we left the paved road. However it felt markedly different on the ground. The gravel road was only just a track, a clearing away of the bigger rocks from a ribbon that stretched hours ahead of us. From time to time we passed an airstrip, with a similar approach to making an elongated space with fewer stones in the middle than on either side.

In my travels I came across a couple from Lancashire who went walking in Iceland in 1931 and recorded their own description of 'a fine example of what by courtesy is called a road. It consisted of a plentiful supply of stones of the most awkward size and shape, over which we stumbled in a careful search for the softest places.'

There had been a grinding noise grumbling out of the rear axle even as the bus designated for the Kjolur route rolled out of Reyjkavik bus station. This bus took its time, ascending the 650m high plateau that was the Kjolur plain and then descending with the same level of grumbling as it had maintained since the smooth suburban roads of Reykjavik. We arrived into Akureyri bus station only 45 minutes behind the timetable, a mixture of the broken side window and some passengers being more observant than others about departure times from our scheduled stops.

There was a character in *Njal's Saga* who was told he would be a great man if he could ride to and from three meetings of the Althing. The magnitude of that test had not been obvious from merely reading the words, while tucked up in the eaves of my Reykjavik guesthouse. Now I had gone by bus through the interior I had reminded myself of what could be involved in riding from one part of the country to another. A walker in 1928 had consoled herself, as she walked from Reykjavik to Akureyri, for her 'slow progress by reflecting that [she] had come to Iceland with the hope of escaping speed, motorcars, and senseless hurry'.

In Akureyri I had planned some time off from MacNeiceing and had two places in particular from my travels in 1986 that I wanted to revisit.

The first of these was the Botanical Gardens of Akureyri.

On the way to the Botanical Gardens, the road, climbing one of Akureyri's hills and looking out across Ejafjordur, was lined by substantial several-storeyed houses. One proclaimed itself to have been built in 1926, another in 1928. Akureyri was far enough from Reykjavik that it was confident in being its own place.

I remembered the Botanical Gardens from 1986 as being marvellously green, in the sense of being to marvel at. In those gardens were the first trees I had seen since leaving home. Now trees are a far more common sight in Iceland, thanks to several very determined reforestation drives spread around the country. The trees in the Botanical Gardens have grown up and filled out into areas of near woodland, but the gardens are still, after journeying through the harsh and stony uplands, an unexpectedly verdant place of lushness. The gardens remain a cared-for, domesticated place. The statues now in the gardens include one added in 1994 to honour all the baby-sitters of Akureyri. Here was a place where the sharpest realities of this glacial-carved landscape, just below the Arctic Circle, might be softened.

I sat for a while, musing on this and that, including whether the flock of sparrow-sized finches with a touch of red might be linnets and if the ones that were very pale might be snow buntings. My bird book gave me no reason to rescind my tentative thought of having seen snow buntings, but cautioned that 'linnet presents many traps for unwary observer' and suggested instead twite or redpoll. Chastened for my unwariness, I inclined cautiously to redpoll, having looked up the maps of what might actually be flying around this far north, even in a Botanical Garden, which has amongst its labelled plants various 'Hardy alien species'.

The other place I wanted to revisit was Husavik, the fishing village, just above 66 degrees north (though still below the Arctic Circle) that had, since my single night camped on its outskirts in 1986, re-invented itself as a place for whale-watching boats.

I booked myself on a day trip of Akureyri's 'Diamond Circle', the response to Reykjavik's 'Golden Circle', and heard from our guide how the rates of suicide and domestic violence in Husavik were those of a place that has something wrong with it.

In my memory the campsite at Husavik was nearly empty. We were glowed upon by a sunny evening, with mountains behind and sea in front, so clear we thought we could see all the way to the island of Grimsey, the Icelandic island that is touched by the Arctic Circle. When I looked back to my 1986 holiday notes, more prosaically I had noted, on the morning after, that 'the fish processing smell prevails, mixed with the sulphur tinge'.

I concluded that Husavik was not a place I could go back to. It was a quiet campsite after several noisy ones. It was a slow and lingering sunset after several evenings of rain. What made Husavik the place that I remembered in 1986 was its context.

So I may need to put into context my eating an ice-cream, in a backstreet of Akureyri, sitting on a bench that was in the sun but probably not in Celsius' double figures (and in the old money of Fahrenheit not quite into the 50s). I was sheltered from the wind enough to have thrown off one of my four layers of clothes. The ice-cream was a milky, rather than creamy, vanilla ice-cream with chocolate chunks and slices of strawberry, but that does not convey the particular joys of that bench outside the Brynja ice-cream shop in Akureyri in the far north of Iceland.

The ice-cream tasted so good in part because of my accidental happening upon it, as my eye was caught by an oversize Arsenal football club Tshirt (a long way from its north London roots) in the window of a neighbouring house. In part the ice-cream tasted so good because I was on holiday. The ice-cream business dated from 1939 and was therefore outside my chosen Icelandic time period. The shop was frequented by a steady stream of locals, even on a non-descript Tuesday afternoon, so I was also part of a community, enjoying the moment.

~

Much more structured than my ambling around the streets of Akureyri was my daytrip around Akureyri's 'Diamond Circle'. We did waterfalls, volcanic craters, mud (both boiling and plopping), sulphur fumaroles and smell-free sea cliffs.

The brochure description was absolutely correct. The tour was 'fully guided'. The guide knew a huge amount (both relevant and not entirely on point) and enjoyed sharing his information and gleaning in turn from us, his clients, more information to add to his stores. It was his way, he said, of lazy travelling, learning about the world without leaving his home country.

The most memorable moments were not the set piece waterfalls or further unique lava formations. The French couple on the tour with me were stopped in their tracks (and came back to it several times in the day) by the guide saying the best way to prepare lamb was to marinade it for four or five days in the fridge. To compound the enormity of this, the guide was also not in favour of using olive oil in his marinades. The French couple could scarcely contain their shocked disbelief as they exclaimed.

Even more memorable to me than watching French marinaded astonishment was the guide's summary of the English language. There were three words which were the most useful. 'Well' because that gave him time to think. 'Stuff' because it could be used in many different replies to nosy 'What are you doing' sort of questions. Stuff helped make answers to send people away to mind their own business. The third most useful word was 'but', because there always was a but. If you started with sun there would be rain, but if you started with rain there would be sun.

On our daytrip we had rain on and off, but mostly on. Yet by our return to Akureyri, we had all enjoyed a day out. I think the word for that day was 'fellowship', a day of sharing experiences, having interesting conversations and within the support (in this case, not the confines) of a day when most decisions had already been taken for us, by the mere fact of signing up for the daytrip.

One conversation among our small group was about why each of us were taking (or not taking) photographs. What did we do with them? Or what, when we were taking them, did we think we were going to do with them? Did we see more because we were looking at the world through the framing device of a camera? Or did we see less because we were concentrating on the view through that lens? Native Icelandic, French, German, Japanese and Chinese speakers all discussed such matters in their second or third language, the only language I can speak.

The guide told us that he, like many in Iceland, claimed their ancestry from the last Catholic bishop of Iceland, who was executed with two of his sons in 1550, a nugget of information, like many that day, that was put out for us, the clients, to pick up or pass by.

The gusting wind wobbled some heavily-laden bicycles in front of the minibus and the guide, driving with a headset adjusted and ready to broadcast his commentary, rightly observed that the roads were not made for bicycling, 'these bicycle people are not my friends'.

The guide took his guiding seriously, though he did admit that although he had discovered in his first full season of guiding that so many women ask so many plant questions he had only got as far as buying a boring plant book last winter. He found it so boring that he had decided to study it next winter.

We could not have a day out in Iceland without some basalt columns and these too were provided by our comprehensive tour guide, at a place signposted as Vestardular. We made our way around and over some slippery rocks in medium-density rain to look at this particular incarnation of basalt columns. All of us, except our guide, were in the separate world provided by the hood of a waterproof and as the rain became more serious only one of our number took photographs to preserve those basalt columns in that medium.

The formation of basalt columns and the glacial action responsible for flat-topped mountains washed over me, a flow of information, cooler and gentler than lava. Some outliers from the guide's commentary lodged with me and others merged into a general sense of being informed.

The pagan's heaven had beer in it, but what if heaven nowadays only has harps and singing? The arctic fox only has a four-day mating season. Mistakes are instruments of learning to be used. There is a type of protein in the milk of the cows that came over to Iceland with the early settlers that is still in the Icelandic cows and protects even fat old farmers from getting the sugar disease of type 2 diabetes. Gay couples in Iceland can share their tax allowances. German girls are very good for Iceland, they come over and look after the Icelandic horses and then fall in love with the Icelandic horse guys who only know about Icelandic horses and the German girls look after the Icelandic horse guys too. Cooking is like music, putting things together which are better together.

Thus the fullness of the guiding bounced along from the serious to the curious, via the scientific explanation and the opinionated joke, all tailored to his audience.

We came to a roadside service area, with fuel for sale on the forecourt and the attraction of flushing toilets in the building behind. There we all enjoyed being stationary, after some hours of gravelled roads. While the Chinese member of our daytrip fellowship sustained herself with a helping of French fries and ketchup I too had a 'Globalised World Moment' when I spotted that the television on the counter was (thanks to the BBC News Channel) telling me about the impressive first innings total being built by the Australian batsman on the first day of the fifth Test match. (This was the final Test match in the series and was being played after the Ashes had been won by England just before my dinner in Hellnar a few days earlier.)

~

At the end of my holiday in Akureyri, my time away from MacNeice, it was cheaper (such is the way of the 21st century) to fly south for an hour from Akureyri to Reykjavik than to catch another bus for a day. For all the warning of light turbulence, it was a smooth and straightforward hop. (I had worried that 'light' turbulence might be like the drenching of 'light' rain I had experienced on my arrival into Iceland at Keflavik airport.)

The current President of Iceland was on my flight from Akureyri. He was a taller man with distinguished white hair. He did have an empty seat next to him at the front of the plane and had a black car waiting to greet him when we touched down in Reykjavik, but he was flying alone, carrying his own bag. For those who had a bag to check in, there were no luggage labels attached because all luggage in Akureyri airport was going to Reykjavik.

The simplicity of the flight south had not prepared me for my next flight, again scheduled to be a short hop, this time to Isafjordur, in the north-west of Iceland. We were due to leave

Reykjavik airport just before 9am, but that got pushed back and pushed back and after an hour the updating announcements themselves were rescheduled to less than hourly.

The approach to Isafjordur involves flying up the fjord, before turning sharply at the head of the fjord and then landing on the runway before it becomes salt water again. For that manoeuvre it is best to be able to see the mountains concerned and see them from both sides of the plane's windows, so we waited for the clouds to lift. I watched the security man setting up his equipment for the international flights to places I now discovered to be in Greenland. I watched those flights go. I watched flights go to every other quarter of Iceland, planes that flew low enough over their potential customers' houses that it was worth painting the airline's website address underneath the plane's body.

The morning shift on the food kiosk took their break and those of us waiting for the clouds to lift in Isafjordur began to recognise each other. One lady with a capacious handbag was more than a third of the way through her equally voluminous paperback thriller by lunchtime. A collection of grey suits of various ages had been drinking beer and consulting their mobile phones, but by lunchtime had decided to leave the airport.

I could have flown on a round trip to Akureyri and back, while I waited for Isafjordur's clouds to lift; instead, introduced by a moment of confusion from an announcement made only in Icelandic, I got talking to another non-Icelandic speaker. Barely 20 she regretted that her French had, in her words, 'gone out the window', since German and English were the languages she spoke most often, after her native Dutch, though her Spanish was enough for a good holiday. As a monoglot I could not really develop that thread of the conversation, so we came back to why we were both in the airport waiting for a flight to Isafjordur.

I told her something about Louis MacNeice and me.

She told me she was a cellist who was about to start her master's degree by attending a week's course a further half an hour's drive north of Isafjordur. This was the first time she had travelled on her own, rather than with a group of others, and more importantly she was worried at the prospect of not travelling with her cello. The airline had insisted the cello could not have its own seat but must travel with the rest of the baggage, so it too had been checked in at 8am for the flight that did not leave at 9am.

By the time I was lunching on a ham roll and bowl of Skyr (an Icelandic variation of yogurt) from the food kiosk I was back to my usual waiting habits. I made a series of lists in my head setting out alternative plans that I might swing into operation, depending on the degree of flight disruption promised by the next postponed announcement. I speculated with the cellist about the backstory of various of those waiting in the airport. Given the width of possibilities encompassed by some of my speculations, the cellist herself speculated that maybe I was really a private detective. That was, I thought to myself, no more unlikely than my being a corporate lawyer and company secretary writing a book about places associated with a dead Irish poet.

We shared a table for the afternoon. When we were not reading or listening to music on our own, we conversed about this and that together. She asked me about my favourite English words. Hers were mischievous and mesmerise, whose sound she enjoyed.

Without giving the question due and proper consideration, I replied that sunshine was one of mine. We agreed that sunshine did not imply warm weather and that some of the best sunshine was that on a crisp autumn day or breaking out to surprise a winter's afternoon. It was a cheerful word, encapsulated in two syllable simplicity. (Given the range of our conversation in English I suspected her French, even if out of the window and lolling around in the garden, was still well able to fend for itself.)

I considered heading down the track of talking about the least favourite words in England of 'rail replacement bus service' but decided that was too close to our current predicament, so instead introduced her to the polite-sounding phrase that camouflaged a bluntly-held opinion 'pusillanimous invertebrate'. There was also the option of categorising a relatively commonly-found phenomenon with the less-commonly used epithet 'bovine defecation'.

The clouds lifted.

The lady from the checkin desk walked through the waiting area collecting the boarding passes from the 9am flight and handing out our new ones.

The flight took off a little after 5pm.

At Isafjordur we landed in a general sense of enveloping embrace as most passengers that Saturday evening had several to greet them. The cellist was reunited with her cello, relieved that the case at least looked unscathed, and she met her contact, ready to drive her onwards to Sudureyri.

There was a faded red minibus that took newspapers and unmet passengers from arriving flights into the centre of Isafjordur. There

I got the keys to another comfortable room in the eaves of a guesthouse; I rashly changed out of my walking boots despite the heavily overcast evening; and I took myself off for a turn about the streets of Isafjordur to clear my lungs of the day of airport air. A car pulled alongside me and asked in deliberate English for my help with directions. Happily they were looking for 'my' guesthouse so I could help, despite this time having been in the town only minutes.

My laptop however pouted unhelpfully in Isafjordur and refused to connect with a network that it said did not meet its expectations. Pressing the inappropriately-styled 'Help' option only brought up the message that, as I was not connected to the internet, I could not be given any help about how to connect in such circumstances to the internet.

This had the benefit of sparing me some of the more grinding aspects of the fifth and final Test match. The soporifically slow over rates and a washed-out day all passed me by and I left, until my return to the eaves of my Reykjavik guesthouse, catching up on the peculiarity that was the measurement of light several days ago, affecting whether the game, days later on the final day, could be played through to a result. It seemed that the regulations meant that the final day was stopped in its tracks by the umpires, with only a handful of overs still left to play. The spectators felt hard done by and England benefited from a 3-0 score in the series, a scoreline that was rather flattering in the circumstances.

When I opened my curtains on my first morning in Isafjordur I too felt rather hard done by, for there, in this hard to reach top left-hand corner of Iceland, wrapped once more in low-cloud that denied even the hint of the mountains that I had seen the night before, was a large cruise ship. When I set off to explore the town, to see its Heritage Museum and find a lunch place from which to watch the rain, there were flocks of British pensioners who had got everywhere before me.

I think the theory was that Isafjordur has houses still standing from the 18th century and plenty of small corrugated iron single-storey homes from the late 19th century, all of which would be most photogenic on a sunny day and might just about pass for being moodily atmospheric on a grey day, but in practice, on an ever wetter day, I gathered bus timetables and tourist office suggestions and then took myself back into my guesthouse eaves to reconsider the day, while the pensioners resolutely 'made the best of it' in sensible shoes and cagoules, even if they were not all entirely sure what It was they were making the best of or indeed where that It was.

From my guesthouse eyrie I watched the last tender of the day ferry the final passengers to the cruise ship and then the various preparations of winching the tenders back on board and closing up the embarkation platforms that folded out from the ship's hull, before she sailed away and the sun came out to show me and the town's population of perhaps 2,700 what the cruise passengers had missed.

The mountains came into view again. The sun picked out an orange edging to the uppermost ridge. The fjord reflected more sharply in the water than it appeared on land, the jumble of man-made and natural features that lined the shore. I, along with a portion of a returning local football team, had rice and a mixture of the more popular dishes from the buffet on offer at the Thai restaurant in the supermarket mall. This restaurant had more ambience than might be expected of such a location, as the Sunday evening regulars came in to pick up their takeaway orders and catch up on the weekend's doings with the footballers and the restaurant staff.

The conclusion I had drawn from the gathered bus timetables and tourist office suggestions was that the summer season was over. The schools had gone back. The bus, ferry and swimming pool timetables were now those for the winter season. The first snows of winter were forecast for the end of the week, just before the next cruise ship came into the fjord.

However it was still August, so there was still the possibility of the sun shining (unlike the two months of the year when the sun does not get above the mountains to shine in to Isafjordur). There was still the last tourist boat of the season, making the half an hour journey from Isafjordur to the 2km long island of Vigur to watch eider ducks and feel eider down.

The sheep on Vigur did seem to be extremely (and preparedly) woolly. I had looked around the display on subsistence farming in the Heritage Museum in Isafjordur. It had extolled the virtues of seaweed grazing for sheep. Like nearly every museum I saw in Iceland the display was labelled in English as well as Icelandic, but despite that I was not entirely sure whether the grazing by the sheep was renowned as being good for the seaweed (with all the sheep droppings fertilising the seaweed) or whether it was the sheep that benefited more from eating the seaweed. Certainly the sheep on Vigur were looking well on their diet.

In the Heritage Museum I was very taken with the Latin name for the Bladder Wrack seaweed being Fucus Vesiculosus, which information was of no possible use to me and not even something I would remember without writing down, but the words did slop around in a most satisfactory way for something of the seashore.

The display on subsistence living also had one of those long-handled poles with a loop on the end that was used in times past for bird-catching. Seeing the length of the pole, the thin flexibility of it, I put myself (in my imagination) with a rope tied round my waist, hanging over a cliff, a strong wind blowing the rain into my face and marvelled how they hooked in any birds at all. Bird-catching was one way to vary the dried fish diet and I could quite understand that there would come a time in the year when a community would want to do that. Seals and whales were, for these small communities, on the fringe of cultivatable land and cliff-defined coast, another way of varying the diet, perhaps even saving them from winter starvation in the lee of a poor harvest.

If a whale did get stranded on the shoreline there were rules about what the person discovering the whale was to do. If they did not either make the whale secure or rush to tell the nearest settlement so the people there could secure the whale, then a fine was imposed. The lawyer in me wondered how you would prove that someone had seen a beached whale that was not secured but that had refloated out into the fjord.

That museum also had a display of piano accordions, more than 50 of them, about which I am no wiser than I was, since there was little labelling in any language. Even without any narrated background the instruments were impressive examples of finely-wrought craftsmanship. Mostly they were in black and white or red and white, but there were some silvery ones with mother of pearl and one very stately instrument in several shades of blue. Each instrument was the epitome of multi-tasking, with piano keys for one hand, small circular keys, often with names like organ stops, for the other hand and in between air to be squeezed in and out. The majority came from Germany or Italy but some said they were made in Sweden. One label did say that a good player might be paid, for a whole evening's playing, only a bag of potatoes. Looking at the problems of growing enough good potatoes to fill a bag in this part of the world, a bag for an evening's tunes did not seem to me to be such an unequal bargain.

The ground floor of the Heritage Museum in Isafjordur was thoroughly imbued with the heritage of the area, that is to say, it smelt very strongly indeed of fish. There were plenty of items from the various stages of the fishing industry and each gave off the smell. By 1930 Iceland had 45 trawlers of its own, which does not seem many if you put them, proverbially, end to end, but it was a huge step up from the farmer in a boat, fishing the coastline of his farm, via the vagaries of sailing boats, to the processing enabled by motor boats and trawlers.

~

My MacNeiceing in Isafjordur had led me into places I had not expected and so for my last afternoon in Isafjordur I opted for a gentle jaunt. I caught the school bus that went up to the head of the fjord (where the airport now looked ready to be a contender for an award for the most scenic location for a commercial airport). The bus dropped off children of all ages at bus stops and street corners that were presumably near their homes.

I wondered if the planting of pansies in Isafjordur took it up to a higher per capita ratio of pansy to population than the previous high-water mark of the pansy plantings in Akureyri.

Then we plunged into a tunnel.

On looking again at my map I could see that the road divided and turned right to Sudureyri. What I had not expected was for that turning to be underground, in the tunnel, and that once the road was no longer going to Flateyri as well, it went down to a single track road, with passing places, still underground, in the tunnel.

When we emerged from the tunnel (of 6km, opened in 1996) the end of the summer in Isafjordur, marked with wispy clouds in a pale blue sky, had turned into the start of winter as we descended the mountain pass to Sudureyri. By the time I got off the bus the prospect of two hours until the returning bus was cold and grey. Still, not to be outdone by British pensioners on a cruise ship outing, I made the best of it, setting a brisk pace out to the origin of the all-pervading fish smell. Fish-processing and fish-handling was the reason for Sudureyri being and yet somewhere in the vicinity I knew there was also a gathering of several dozen music students from across Europe, including a Dutch cellist, all starting their new academic year.

I tried a few side streets, down to the fjord and back, and watched some of the fish-related activity between a fork-lift truck and a container-loaded lorry. The grey sky was getting darker, but I was cheered to discover that the winter timetable then in force meant the swimming pool had just opened, moments before I reached its front door.

Despite not finding my time in The Blue Lagoon the most relaxing, I had persevered with one of the favourite relaxations of Icelanders (not least as it usually cost less than a cup of coffee) and gone to the swimming pools in Akureyri and Reykjavik. Now in Sudureyri, although there was no one in the changing room to follow, I felt I knew my way around the protocols of Icelandic swimming pools.

First stop was to leave your shoes on the racks outside the changing room (unless you had brought a bag to put them in, which would also fit in the locker with your clothes). Sudureyri had the shoe racks outside the changing room but no lockers. Clothes could be hung up on hooks and valuables given to the lifeguards who took the ticket money from those who did not have passes. I hung my clothes up and hoped I had not chosen someone else's favourite hook.

I located the towel rack, put my towel in it, awaiting my return and positioned far enough away from the spray of the showers, and then turned to the showers themselves. Some pools had had push buttons that assumed what was the right temperature and turned off the water after their allotted time. In Sudureyri there were hot and cold taps on each shower to be adjusted, but adjusting the first one brought no water. Maybe you needed to be nearer the door at the start of the session? I tried a shower diagonally opposite the first shower. Still no water. Thinking of Einstein and madness being doing the same thing repeatedly and expecting a different result, I looked around before trying a third shower.

'Eureka' (yes I know that was not Einstein and it applied to jumping out of a bath, not into a shower), there it was, a master button that, once pushed, set running both of the showers whose taps I had twiddled and several whose taps I had not touched. By the time I had turned off all the showers I was not intending to shower under and adjusted to a suitable temperature the shower I was intending to use, I was not nearly completed with all the designated washing, when the master button cut off the water.

There had been posters in The Blue Lagoon, Reykjavik and Akureyri to illustrate what should be washed before entering the pools; in Sudureyri there were no posters, knowledge was assumed. Once washed as designated and dressed for the swimming pool I ventured forth, through the heavy wooden door to the outside, for which I was not dressed.

Earlier in the day the outside temperature had been on display in Isafjordur, but I suspected it was colder in later afternoon Sudureyri than 9C (48F). Brisk and purposeful steps took me straight into the main pool, a short 16m pool that made me feel as if my lengths were more energetic than they were. The darkening grey sky was now letting drop a fine drizzle, which I could ignore as I gently progressed to and fro in solitary state. For the winter the pools were shut on Monday and Friday, but opened for three hours from 4pm in the middle of the week, allowing for a swim (and probably also a soak in the hot pots) after school or work. The pools were also open from 10am to 3pm at the weekend.

Having done the equivalent of eat some plain bread and butter sandwiches, with lengths of there and back swimming, I moved from the main rectangular pool to the small circular hot pot, the sticky chocolate cake course of luxuriating idly in the warmth.

Sudureyri was another of Iceland's geothermally-heated pools. The water was regulated to a constant temperature in the hot pots, though what that temperature was might vary a little between one day and the next. The sign by the hot pot I sampled said 40C (over 100F). There was no doubt that, of the options I had found in Sudureyri, I was in the best place to pass the time before the return bus to Isafjordur.

Being in warm water already it was surprisingly soothing to feel the rain on my face. For once 'just about keeping my head above water' had very positive connotations.

A flustered white wagtail ran and stopped and ran again along the edge of the main pool, then paused once more, before flying, at quite a steep angle, up to catch an insect.

Soaking in an Icelandic hot pot may not be a traditional bird-watching hide, but the same principles apply: find your location, sit quietly in it making very little movement, watch what passes by.

As there was no one else in the hot pot I could sit where I liked and not trouble myself about the etiquette of where you sit in a part-full hot pot. The starting point seemed to be, as it was on entering a part-full Northern Line carriage, to aim for a bisection of the available empty space. On the Northern Line there is not then the added complication of whether there is sufficient space, within the boundaries of a convention I only dimly grasped, to stretch out my feet, instead of keeping them tidily tucked in.

In the hot pot I sampled in Reykjavik the soakers already there had their legs stretched out, almost like the teeth of a zip, so (happily for a lawyer) I had a precedent to follow. All of a sudden something one lady said caused her listener to ground her feet and turn round and look at the speaker in astonishment, which led to a domino of other legs being tucked in out of the way.

There was a second slightly less crowded hot pot in Laugardalslaug, the biggest of the swimming pools in Reykjavik, but that seemed exclusively occupied by male grey hairs of sufficient uniformity that I decided not to interrupt what might have been a meeting of a local retired businessmen's association.

The other twist in the hot pots in Reykjavik was that one (the one I tried) had artistically placed rocks and various points of entry, so the soaker might not spot that someone they were not wishing to see was not only there and unseen, but perhaps hearing any gossip being shared by the soaker with the person they had come to the hot pot to see and share gossip with.

When I had been soaking quietly in the hot pot in Akureyri I did wonder about the etiquette of what is shared in a hot pot, where a soaker is nearer to listening neighbours than in a coffee shop. There was a gentle murmur of catching up going on around me, an Icelandic aural backdrop, until it was punctuated by two of my fellow soakers suddenly breaking into English and then I could not help but hear everything they were saying, because the English overlaid the Icelandic, even though they were not addressing the pool stridently.

~

In the grey early evening there was me and a teenager in a grey hooded top waiting at the bus stop in Sudureyri. The teenager's cigarette lighter was running low, not helped by the swirling wind that had not made up its mind about the direction it would blow in. The teenager persisted in trying to light his cigarette, even when he answered his phone and tucked that between ear and neck. I did wonder whether he might set fire to his hood, but the bus arrived before I could find out and before he could start puffing on his cigarette.

Back we went to the relative metropolis of Isafjordur, where family groups were out on the path parallel to the main road, preparing their winter fitness on cross-country length skis mounted on roller-skates. There was a gym round the corner from my guesthouse that advertised opening hours of 0540 to 2100 during the week, but on Sundays 1300 to 1600. (Sunday mornings were for whatever mixture of church, family and hangovers was appropriate.)

The story was told of a man from Westfjord coming into a shop. 'How are you?' asked the shopkeeper. 'Very well, very well,' replied the customer. 'That's good to hear', said the shopkeeper, 'when you walked in I thought perhaps you were limping a bit.' 'Oh yes, I am,' replied the customer, 'but only when I walk.'

The impression I left Iceland with in 2013, was not much changed from that of 1986, and I suspect had much in common with that formed by its visitors in 1936. Iceland still projected itself as a self-sufficient place, despite being buffeted by weather and by some of the more extreme forces of nature. Her people got on with what mattered to them, through boom and bust, and if they had any complaints they would not be sharing them with foreigners.

Foreigners would remember the rain, but brighter would be their memories of stark landscapes, illuminated with ever-changing light.

Three weeks in a country gave an impression, a partial and superficial impression that made writing about it much easier than distilling a longer and deeper experience. As the birds started to sing again in south London, with the cooling of summer I typed one word after another, in the order that seemed to me suitable. From my distance I built my impressions of Iceland and then reread them. Was my Iceland a northern place others would recognise?

~

Westward was another island, one that I had put off writing about, delaying my visit until the heat had gone out of their summer.

The death of Seamus Heaney, Nobel laureate and Irish poet, brought Ireland back into the headlines and for better than usual reasons. A selection of his poems (read by him) was broadcast by the BBC in celebration of his life. His *Shipping Forecast* included a 'sibilant penumbra' as the last shipping forecast of the day was read. All is not dark. There is a place sibilant with vowels and consonants, a place where the song of language lilts and smiles, just slightly.

MacNeice was born in Belfast. He grew up just beyond there in Carrickfergus and his family's roots were in Connemara in the west.

I never had any intention of going everywhere that MacNeice went. Leaving Greece and (after some consideration) Ghana to others; skipping Spain; ignoring India and swathes of countries further East were pragmatic decisions based on my budget of time and money. Those were just some of the places he passed through, but Ireland, with all its history of fraught contradictions and difficulties of definition, was his home for the first third of his life. Throughout his life Ireland was where he had come from. Even if others forgot or never knew, he was always Irish.

Sitting in my garden, I was surprised by a fluffy flock of long-tailed tits, less dapper than earlier in the year and busying themselves to no apparent purpose in my pyracanthus, unintimidated by its thorns.

I enumerated arguments to myself. I had planned my travelling to places that had MacNeice connections, but I had chosen those places to be places I could enjoy writing about in a way that readers might enjoy reading about. Did I have to enjoy both the travelling and the writing? Certainly I did not have to enjoy the sensation of rain-sodden trouser legs, but if I wrote about wet trouser legs there had to be enough of interest to me (before the words reached any other reader) that would survive editing and proofreading, long after the trousers themselves had dried out.

Separated by a consonant my writing about Ireland after Iceland would be surrounded by the baggage I already had. I grew up with the steady stream of BBC news bulletins about those things that were reported from Northern Ireland. When I moved to work in central London IRA bombs blasted out my employer's windows, twice.

The long-tailed tits made the clicking noises of very small pebbles telling each other off. Right I told myself. Time to get back to work. Time to book my writing visit to Northern Ireland and to the Republic of Ireland.

~

I went there.

I came back.

Now I am continuing to type.

My previous six months of typing have taught me that first I must type, after that I can edit, self-censor or delete completely.

~

My visits to Northern Ireland and to the Republic of Ireland were shorter than my writing visit to Iceland. I was consciously superficial, focused on specifically selected pinpricks of MacNeice connection.

I visited three MacNeice addresses in Northern Ireland and drove myself in a rented car through two Connemara places in the Republic of Ireland that would have been names spoken of as home by MacNeice's father and mother.

I looked inside two Church of Ireland churches: one in Clifden, Connemara, where Louis MacNeice's parents were married, the other in Carrickfergus where his father was Rector.

Walking beyond that second church I came upon a black and white mural, stark in the painted freshness of its demarcation. I took no photographs. I walked on. The masked gunman of the mural watched me.

~

Where to start?

I can only describe what I saw.

The head was dark, somewhere between grey and green. Below the head there was a white neck band, not exactly a clerical collar as it did not go all the way round. The body was brown. The upper part was the miscellaneous freckled brown of any number of birds in the 'little brown job' section of my bird book and the lower part was a redder brown. The small bird was waiting for something of interest to pass by and I was not that, so it did not move from its perch in the upper reaches of the brambles beside the road that led down to The Giant's Causeway, the UNESCO world heritage site on the north Antrim coast of Northern Ireland.

It was not a robin, but was of a similar size and was watching with that same alertness, in the unlikely event I did something useful.

Despite my summer not being short of basalt columns I had chosen to take time out from MacNeiceing and add some more basalt columns to my collection. Instead of looking up at towering Icelandic basalt columns, in Northern Ireland I could walk across their tops. Here Finn McCool took the legendary responsibility for their formation, striding across to Scotland for an altercation with a fellow giant, the Scottish Fingal (of Fingal's Cave on the Hebridean island of Staffa). Alternatively, as in Iceland, these columns too were formed from volcanic eruptions millions of years ago.

Both versions of their creation were laboriously retold on an audioguide that had been recorded to satisfy a consultant's definition of the Irishness expected by the target tourist market.

I might be a tourist, but I was not from the continent of the target market. What might seem charmingly local when delivered in person, was gratingly contrived in its digital incarnation. Stories about names given to rock formations burbled on, only to be lengthened by witterings about possible nicknames for the fictional guide. Happily the battery soon went flat.

Sea-watching. People-watching. Bird-watching. Elements of a Saturday afternoon off.

~

'Contentment is Wealth' said the pedestal of a sculpture in the centre of Ennis, the county town of Clare in the Republic of Ireland.

The shops in Ennis had names that were descriptive, not names that were bland in 28 countries. A clothes shop had clothes in its name. Like all its neighbours, its window display was dressed in blue and yellow, for blue and yellow were the colours of County Clare and County Clare was in the 2013 All-Ireland Hurling final. Several shops were shut with a handwritten sign in the window 'Gone Hurling'. Others had a typed sheet advising they would be shutting earlier than usual.

As I bought a sandwich two women behind me in the queue hoped there would be a result this time, in the replayed final. Their men and children had gone again to Dublin this weekend too and what with the tickets for the game, the transport and all the rest, it was getting expensive.

The streets emptied. By five o'clock everyone had found a television.

Where to start?

I had never seen hurling before. Two teams of 15 on a rugby-sized pitch, clashing sticks together to pull the ball away like a hockey game, flicking a ball off the ground like a lacrosse game, only taking a few steps before moving the ball like a basketball game, running at sprinters' speeds with the ball held out far in front of them on their stick like an egg and spoon race, barging the opposition as footballers might try, throwing the ball with the speed and accuracy of a cricketer's throw, tossing the ball up and walloping it with their stick and the ferocity of a frustrated tennis-player's smash - all to get the ball into the net of a goal, or less valuably over the goal's crossbars, but between the rugby-like uprights, for a point.

Clare last won the final in 1997, but they had won the under-21s final the week before so they had, or so it was agreed in Ennis, momentum. Clare started the game by demonstrating a variety of different ways in which both goals and points can be scored. Cork were on the pitch, but it took them longer to start playing.

Once Cork did start playing, the noise levels rose beyond the very loud. Clare's lead started to slip through the fingers. Eight points ahead halved to four points by half time. Cork inched up to parity.

Ennis inhaled.

Scores started to pull Clare ahead again.

I admired the TV commentators avoiding any mention of the fat lady singing as the minutes of the second half ticked down. A 19-year old wrote himself into the mythology of All-Ireland finals by scoring a hat-trick of Clare goals when he had not been in the starting lineup for much of the season. I appreciated the grounded reality of the commentator: this bright afternoon may overshadow the rest of the young lad's life. How does this afternoon's hero step down from this teenage pinnacle and out onto the training pitch at the start of the next season, weighed down by 82,000 memories of those who watched his every step in today's stadium?

Another Clare goal as injury time faded.

A famous victory sealed.

'They hurled their hearts out,' said the commentator. A new usage to me of the verb.

There was a quietness on the streets of Ennis, a collective exhaling.

For a few moments, all was still.

Then the pavements whooped and the narrow streets of Ennis were full of carhorns.

~

Another day. Another bar. Another place where I did not know the language.

I was perched on a bar stool. It was the last day of the Clifden Arts Festival week at the end of September and in the interval between two sets of traditional music, a poet was reading his work. The soft Irish sounds soothed, though they might have been describing anguished pain. The poet's language changed to English. The audience listened intently, waiting for the music to resume before buying another round of drinks.

After appreciative applause, violin, accordion and guitar filled the low-ceilinged bar. My feet did not reach the bar stool's crossbar, so they waggled, rather than tapped, to the music. (One of the hamlets I had passed through on my drive over to Clifden had begun its list of attractions painted on a wall with the headline: 'Beer, Books'.)

Words and alcohol, in varying proportions, flowed.

～

Home again I concluded that the bird in the brambles above The Giant's Causeway had been a stonechat.

I printed out some snapshots of the addresses and churches I had visited. Each illustrated a moment in a place, but no more. There was a penumbra around each.

Now the season for basalt columns was over. London was patchworked in umbrellas. The tourist flocks had thinned.

This autumn was no different from past autumns. Berries swelled. Pigeons pecked on the orange berries of my pyrancanthus.

This October was different for me. I saw it, fragmenting from generalist greens into each particular shade of passing. The last rose petal slipped to earth and I noticed the starkness of the unclothed twigs.

The year continued.

I had one more writing visit to plan.

10

Autumn unpacking and repacking

Planning is something I have always done. I subscribe to the truism that, even if the plan turns out to have been useless, the planning, of the useless plan, will have been useful.

I pulled out a sheet of blank paper.

Even a blank sheet of paper has edges. Those edges demarcate what I am not doing and when I am not doing it. Those boundaries keep me from oscillating in perpetual possibility.

There were three months until the end of the calendar year and then three more months until the end of my writing year. I had set aside those last three months for the production phase, so the initial writing had to be done by the year's end and that meant December needed to be earmarked for writing, not travelling.

I marked out on my blank sheet of paper:

> January to March – Edit, typeset, proofread etc
>
> December – Writing about November
>
> November – Experiencing November
>
> October – Writing about September (Ireland) and planning for November

That made it clear. I was already sitting in October. I needed to get on with the job of planning my next writing visit.

From spending time in the footnotes and appendices of books on Louis MacNeice I had discovered that, as well as the major holding of documents in the University of Texas in Austin, there were various MacNeice-related papers and letters held in a number of other universities and institutions.

The BBC website made it very clear that its written archives would not be a place I (an outsider, with no traditional publisher lined up and no academic accreditation for my project) could visit. The BBC was not alone. Other publically-funded British institutions took the same view, that their resources are too scarce to use on outsiders who are, by their very definition, people kept out, herded into a conveniently unexamined lump of otherness.

Happily the most interesting archives for my purposes were held by state universities in the US where the presumption to requests for access from the general public was 'Yes', even requests made by a member of the general public who was a citizen and taxpayer of a foreign country.

While sitting at home in south London (although I am far from being a digital native), the internet enabled me to discover more information more easily than would have been possible even five years ago. I could check the opening times of the various libraries I was interested in visiting, where they were on their respective campuses and perhaps search their catalogue listings. A few more clicks brought up an email address or an information request webpage and from there it was only a little more typing to ask whether the papers and materials I had seen mentioned in

MacNeice footnotes and appendices were still in the same places.

Each of my exploratory emails to the US (to librarians or curators or archivists or wherever the website trail led) received a reply. They were informative replies, often expanding on the detail I had and frequently written in a tone of welcome, a warm welcome to the world of Research, a less-visited place than some of the others I had been to in my writing year, but a place none the less.

Having read *Letters from Iceland* in Iceland, the idea of reading MacNeice's notes made in Iceland had especial appeal. I began my planning of my November writing visit by looking into the practicalities of getting myself to Buffalo, or more particularly to The Poetry Collection of the State University of New York on the North Campus, where the exercise book of MacNeice's notes made in Iceland had lived for decades.

The more I thought about it, the more the idea of Buffalo appealed. It was not a famous city and the land of the not famous is where I live. The pull of Iceland was strong. Iceland was the first place I had visited because of the MacNeice connection. (My visit in 1986 was so far away that the plane there had had a smoking section.) Iceland in 2013 had been the place where, more than any other visited in my writing year, I had read MacNeice's words of the place in the place. Starting and finishing with Iceland, by way of Buffalo, had a symmetry for me (and it was suitably improbable).

The more obvious symmetry, I had to admit, would have been to start with birth and end with death. MacNeice's place of birth had been an accident of his father's job in Belfast and his place of burial in Carrowdore, also in Northern Ireland, was there because that was where his mother was buried. Carrowdore was where his mother was on holiday with her own father when he died and needed burying, so when the time came she was buried there, and therefore that was where Louis MacNeice was buried.

Having the luxury of 'my book, my rules' I decided to ignore the obvious and end my travelling at the mid-point of MacNeice's life. (Well the mid-point if I allowed myself some poetic rounding. MacNeice died just before his 56th birthday and he was 28 during 1936, the year he visited Iceland.) I would travel to Buffalo, that was the answer to 'Where next?'

If Buffalo was the answer, then some people might suggest I was asking the wrong question.

Buffalo had a reputation for being a shrunken city, left behind when its heavy industries closed decades ago, frozen with many months of snow and ice, shared with its near neighbours in Canada. Still it was not as if I was a tourist going on a long-anticipated annual holiday and then choosing to spend it in Buffalo. Other cities have shinier tourist sights and infinitely more famous names than Buffalo, but after a couple of emails I knew I could see in Buffalo what I could not see in any other city. I was going to Buffalo to visit The Poetry Collection.

Certainly I was conscious that if Buffalo was the answer to 'Where', that did narrow down 'When'. I needed to be away from US airports before the mass circulation of population that marks Thanksgiving and the last week of November. That reduced the length of November for raw material gathering. There was another date that was relevant, but it was not a fixed date. It was the date when the snow comes to Buffalo. While Buffalo itself does not blink when its expected snow starts to arrive, it would keep things simpler for me if I left town before wind chill started to matter.

So working backwards from Buffalo I returned to my less blank sheet of paper.

From London to Buffalo I would be flying either by way of Chicago or by way of New York. Chicago was short on MacNeice connections, whereas New York had at least two.

Some more mousing around the internet and I found Columbia University on New York's Upper West Side had transcripts of recordings of reminiscences of many of MacNeice's friends and BBC colleagues which had formed a BBC radio programme called *Louis MacNeice: A Radio Portrait*. Columbia also had a random collection of 38 books that had once been owned by MacNeice. On its website Columbia (as a private university) did not have an obvious presumption to archive requests from the general public of 'Yes,' but when I emailed and explained what I was hoping to look at I got an informative reply and was accorded entry with the status of 'Independent Researcher'.

MacNeice had twice been a visiting lecturer. In 1954 he was at Sarah Lawrence College, half an hour's train ride from New York's Grand Central Station, and the archivists there emailed me back with a list of what I could read in their reading room. My November plan was coming together.

MacNeice's other visiting lectureship had been in 1940 at Cornell University, on the hillside above Ithaca, which in 1940 had been another train ride from Grand Central, but was now a three-hour bus ride from Buffalo and nearer five hours by bus from New York. Putting Buffalo, Ithaca and New York City in a line and calling them an itinerary had an internal logic.

Some more internet mousing and, along with a feeling that the trip was meant to be, I got an email back from the place on Cornell campus where MacNeice had stayed as a guest, confirming that I too could come and stay as a guest.

My blank sheet of paper was filled in.

~

There is a pleasure in things being seasonal. There is a time for conkers and a time for snowballs; a time for strawberries and a time for mince pies. It is true that the commercial infrastructure of supermarkets can now fly the seasons round the world, but a commoditised tradition detached from its place in the calendar withers without its roots. Easter eggs are not the same in Lent.

The Proms season had finished in London's Royal Albert Hall and the swallows (gathered briefly on the phone lines) had gone. Some swans flew overhead, returning from their summer season away.

The passing of the seasons was a reminder that good things come to an end and may (on an optimistic day) be replaced by even better things. Looking out, over my repaired flat roof, the puddles remaining were just enough for sparrows to drink from. The leaves in south London had turned brighter.

I had put summer (where applicable, washed and mended) away. Spiders re-colonised my garden chairs and, beyond my 2013, back in the corporate world, it was the season for budgets and strategic planning, for attaching figures to visions.

I too, in my writing year out of the corporate world, had a budget and a plan, an imagined way of getting from blank computer screen to printed book, via a writer by the name of Louis MacNeice. I too joined in the pretence that spreadsheets have the answers. I looked again at my budget of time and money, the numbers I had speculatively attached to the words of what I wanted to achieve in my writing year. The difference this year was that I could make adjustments to my budget without following any procedure for reporting them. This year what went into my diary was what I put into it, but that also meant that my day no longer had the collegiate community of shared running jokes with work colleagues or an unexpected slice of someone else's birthday cake in the office kitchen. That world went on, without me.

For me the autumn has always been more of a time for reflection than January. (That is partly a relic from years of school and university timetables; partly the result of the more recent working reality of sharply increasing workloads in the first months of the year, that leave no time unaccounted for.)

The 50th anniversary of Louis MacNeice's death in September 1963 had passed, with, it had seemed, scarcely a media ripple. Now I was more than halfway into my writing year, it all began to feel more serious. Previously I was seeing if I could write a book; now the emphasis had shifted. I had spent six of my months. I had not yet written a book.

I felt an obligation to do MacNeice justice. While a job in the corporate world could be done by different people in their different ways, I knew that this writing could only be done by me. I was not writing a book that someone else would write differently. I was writing a book about me and MacNeice and my travelling with him. It was a book that only I could write.

The filled-in sheet of paper that was formerly blank now set me a timetable. The logic of my November itinerary (and the weight of my sense of obligation to be discharged) pushed me towards my habit of being focused on task, doing that which is required, without deviation into byways. When things get constrained, I put my head down and get on with It, whatever that It is.

I took a step back and revisited my timetable for November. My friends were right to suggest putting 'Enjoy' as an entry in its own right on each timetable I drew up, to balance the reality of my default setting.

I put into my November itinerary some 'just in case' time. I allocated some unallocated time for byway deviation, conscious of the oxymoron of structuring spontaneity.

~

I had unpacked my bag from Ireland but testing out various permutations of words to describe my visit there was less straightforward.

Instead I succumbed to the displacement activity of making a list of what to pack for my November trip to New York and of reading around to remind myself of what I should be looking for when I was there, in my time and in MacNeice's.

Life is simpler in one time zone at once, but for most of my writing year I had spent time in MacNeice's past, while writing up, in my present, what I had previously planned to do in what had only recently been the future.

Being in three timeplaces every week becomes dizzying.

With all the unpacking and repacking, the past, present and future nested within my handwritten notes and printed-out sheaves of paper, I was feeling the need to flex my diary and insert some time that was mine, not MacNeice's.

I needed to pause and spend some time in my own personal present.

I chose to spend some of that time, besuited in the specificity of legal update seminars, enjoying analysis of the particular. Are there no rhetorical questions?

One legal seminar morning had been prefaced, coffee cup in hand, by someone telling me how inspirational I was. I had squirmed under the embarrassed weight of such an adjective. Inspirational was for dead figures in history or perhaps for long-retired school teachers.

Could I swop inspirational for another adjective? How about disciplined? That was an adjective I could wear. The word count did not accumulate all by itself; I sat down to type every morning, ignoring (mostly) the array of modern displacement activities that the internet can now offer, as well as the more traditional ones of another song on the radio or even, in an extremity, the displacement from writing providing by doing the washing-up.

On the Northern Line home from that seminar, I did take myself to task. Who was I to suppose what might or might not inspire another person? If my doing something mildly improbable, nudged someone else into getting around to trying out something long-meant to, then good for them trying it, whatever the It was that they tried and whatever the route by which they came to try it. I knew that my squirming was illogical, since I wanted the Proper Book and indeed this, the Other Book, to give its readers ideas, perhaps even ideas that were so big they could, with a straight face, be called inspirational. It was just that inspiration at a distance, the distance of a book's length, or two, was what I had in mind, not inspiration in person and face to face.

If my words gave out some light, then I would much prefer, for myself, to sit away from the words and under the nearest bushel. (Or, on second thoughts, perhaps I should sit further away, under a more distant bushel, leaving the words that once were mine to do their own thing, shedding light or inspiring or flickering out, as a reader might decide.)

Coming back to my personal present I went out for a proper walk and I left MacNeice at home. For ten miles he was not mentioned, because I had not introduced him to my fellow walkers. We spoke of the Here and Now. Was it a buzzard calling from that top field? Did the lunchtime pub open before noon?

~

I took a weekday morning away from the keyboard and went out to watch other people work. An assortment of students, retired folks and I, sat in a concert hall's shadows and watched a mid-morning rehearsal of an orchestra that was to give a concert that evening. For the Royal Festival Hall in London, the concert was part of a series of themed concerts given by a variety of orchestras and soloists; for the orchestra, London was just one stop on a European tour and for them a 15-concert tour meant day after day of different lighting systems.

The first question to be addressed was not one of musical interpretation or tempi, but of lighting and where the shadows fell. The lights of London were shining too brightly and reflecting awkwardly.

And then people got to work. From the anonymous darkness I watched and drifted into thoughts lead by the music.

The rehearsal paused for a break. Someone ate a banana, another had questions about a future visa, a third retired to the stalls to practise some more. Those in search of a fag break collected themselves outside the hall. The conductor left the stage slowly enough to be interrupted by questions, musical or logistical.

Then the orchestra's Friday morning work resumed and a phone, untended in the break, went off.

There was an unspoken pause. The power of silence hung in the air, the power of the space between one sound and another.

Work resumed.

The ensemble playing of violins or horns may be the signature of a symphony orchestra, but there is more to any orchestra than just one section. There is wide scope for metaphor and analogy in the coming together of different instruments from different sections, each of which can only play its own part and must rely on others to play theirs.

Some words of Mary Parker Follett, writing too early in the 20th century to be as widely celebrated as her observations on management deserve, came to my mind. For her, conflict was not inherently a bad thing, there were different types of friction and one skill was knowing which friction to eliminate and which to capitalise on. 'All polishing is done by friction,' she had written. 'The music of the violin we get by friction.'

For Follett, applying domination or compromise to conflict was less likely to lead to a permanent resolution of the conflict, than understanding what common root might lie beneath the conflict and integrating those common roots in the solution.

The presenting symptoms might be noise, not the key to the cure.

The violins played again a requested phrase. The conductor turned to separate out some bars of the woodwind.

For the time being, I thought to myself, I am writing my words for my book, but to reach an audience I will need to work with others and, having auditioned them, will have to rely on them. The conductor plays no instrument and can not see the audience, but is given licence by the orchestra to tell it, with two hands and two feet on slightly higher ground, what to do. The risks of not being able to hear the music when you are inside it, of not being able to tell which words clunk and which glide, punctuated my reverie as the conductor turned to her assistant in the stalls, the person checking the balance of the orchestra's sound. The assistant gave a thumbs-up and before I could hop back onto my train of thought the conductor declared, 'Thank you everyone. See you this evening.'

It was the time to stop.

The rehearsal was like revising for exams, some wanted to carry on tinkering, just a transition here or a key change there. The time will come for me when it will be time to stop revising, no more tinkering with tenses here and there. The time when, as

Winston Churchill once wrote about correcting page proofs, 'We have reached the moment when one must say, "As the tree falls, so shall it lie".' It will then be for the audience to hear whatever music is in my words.

I had gone out to spend a morning on my own and yet MacNeice and writing the Proper Book had still come with me.

~

The time came to practise again releasing words of mine into the outside world. I sent out another newsletter.

It reminded me of reading aloud to the Mat on the tour bus as we straightened up for the Reykjavik road home. On the bus I had read some excerpts from MacNeice's *Letters from Iceland*. I had talked into a microphone and got no reaction from the road ahead, nor could I see whether my words reached the seats behind me.

My newsletter went out, beyond my field of vision.

As an attachment to a list of blind-copied addressees, my newsletter might well fall at the first firewall; it might be inadvertently deleted while looking for something else or it might be left with an unfulfilled intention to be read while waiting to pick up a child or an undelivered parcel. Or my newsletter might distract someone from what they should be doing, perhaps offering a couple of smiles and a snippet of mildly interesting trivia in recompense for the delayed task in hand.

I sent my words out on their own and I turned back to my afternoon of planning November.

I released from my desk a flock of enquiring emails. Then,

before the daylight of that day faded, I switched my laptop off and went out, walking nowhere in particular, looking at fallen leaves and still-flowering front gardens, at over-flowing skips and the mystical patterning of spray-painted symbols that precede yet another hole being dug for one of the utility companies.

There was still a slight warmth in the sun, but the startling intensity of July 2013 was past. The forecast now included regular rain, at frequent, showery intervals – except on the days when it was forecast to rain all day. My umbrella was back ready for duty at the front door, which was as it should be. The calendar and thermometer agreed that it was autumn.

I found some leaves to scuff. They were not as deeply piled nor as crisply curled as is preferable for ideal scuffing, but it was still a seasonal pleasure to be enjoyed. The reality of that particular afternoon was that the season of autumn was being presented, at least that day, with an unbroken grey sky and was, in defiance of stereotypes of mellow fruitfulness, subtitled Dank.

'*Solvitur ambulando*'.

Whether the idea was first formulated by Saint Augustine or by someone else, it is a sound one, the idea of solving things by walking. It is not that all problems can be solved by walking away from them, but there does, more often than not, come a point when sitting looking at something does not improve it.

In April there had been an expanse of alternatives, stretching to the horizon, and now, even with the 'just in case' time inserted into my November itinerary, the width had narrowed.

I did not know what else I would have seen if I had chosen other places to visit; or what conversations I would have had if I had extended my remit beyond places to people. I would never know how much I would have written if I had decided not to be an itinerant outsider but to bring myself under an academic umbrella.

But there comes a time to get up and walk away from What If and Maybe.

I carried on walking and shook the kaleidoscope into a new set of shapes, seeing what was there in a different light.

I remembered how the unlabelled corner of an Austin suburb became a welcome sign of home on my daily bus ride back from the Texan reading room. I remembered how my insignificance became smaller still on the surface of the north Atlantic. There were the coffee tables I watched from in Oxford and Birmingham and the picnic table in the sunshine where I savoured summer in an ice-cream in Iceland. The novelty of identifying a stonechat and watching a hurling match came from places I would not have visited but for their MacNeice connection. All of those places came in to, and out of, focus, as I walked. They were now places that I had known and would remember after I had left this writing year.

I continued on my walk and thought of the less-publicised 'five a day'. (In the UK 'five a day' has been a well-known strapline to encourage five portions of fruit or vegetables to be eaten each day for physical wellbeing.) There had been a UK government-commissioned paper suggesting the five a day for mental wellbeing: Exercise, Give, Connect, Learn and Notice. While not ignoring apples and carrots, and indeed keeping up with the broccoli as well as treating myself to a peach or a kiwifruit from time to time, the mental five a day were no less important, supplying a mixture of the inward (notice and learn) and the outward (give and connect) bound in with the ancient wisdom of a healthy mind in a healthy body, ignored as old-fashioned at our peril. Giving may be a one-way action, done to someone else, but connecting is more often a receiving, an acceptance of someone else's giving, preceded by a noticing, a lifting up of the eyes, risking the unexpected, a disruption to a tightening schedule. Learning may be new, but noticing is often looking properly at the older.

There are some years where the autumn's leaves are swept away before I even notice I have not scuffed them. Some summers are so spent in air-conditioned meeting rooms that on even the hottest days I take a jacket to work.

2013 was not such a year. It was time spent in daylight and in travelling in plain sight. (I had opted out of the proper Travelling that Ghana might have been.) I went to places that people had heard of, that people can find on a map. I got off a bus in Austin at the wrong stop. I sat in an airport all day watching people while cloud did not lift in Iceland. I had conversations with bus drivers and taxi drivers; with tour guides and tourist information staff; with people while they were waiting for something else. We spoke about whether the morning rush hour was usually this slow or what was there before the new flats went up or whether the forecast for the weekend was any better. Despite the answers there was plenty of sunlight, it was just that some of it came with rainbows.

Now I had formulated the plan for my last writing visit. All the things I was not doing were no longer my concern. It was time to concentrate on what I was doing. I was going back to the

US, flying both ways, as conventional early 21st century travellers do. I had made arrangements for my November to start with two weeks of browsing in places that had MacNeice connections, English-speaking places. This militated against the possibility of my writing travel literature that filed itself tidily; to do that, I should have travelled clockwise around one single country or perhaps alphabetically through an entire continent (but only one).

Putting one foot in front of another, I indulged in a modicum of existentialist angst about what, exactly, I was writing. (That 'exactly' should be spoken with considerable stress on the first syllable, combined with a lengthening sense of doubt opened out by the second syllable, but crisply dismissed by the final syllable.)

Having proclaimed at the outset that the Proper Book was not a comprehensive biography and that I am partial, because I admire the poetry and choose to gloss over some of the private detail of the poet, I can not attach the label 'Biography' to the Proper Book. Would it be allowed, despite the country-hopping, to slip in to 'Travel writing' as long as it wore the undifferentiated label 'general'? What about a cross-genre hybrid of 'Travel biography'? (Maybe not. Cross-genre had undertones of an adult gift section; though on second thoughts my local supermarket has a whole section labelled 'adult cereals', so perhaps travel biography could be a cross-genre without descending into dubious double-entendres?)

What about this, the Other Book? It is still a paraquel. It is still going to the same places as the Proper Book, but not seeing all the same things and not always following the same route. The Other Book too may be a candidate for 'Travel writing – general'. That way the two books would stay together, but would they be better each with their own space?

With cricket woven into its fabric could this, the Other Book, keep its end up in conversation with more obviously Ashes-related books on the shelf labelled 'Sports'? No, this, the Other Book, has never played any cricket that required wearing shoes clicking on a pavilion floor.

Or there again, because bird-watchers are a community that help novices, perhaps this, the Other Book, could gatecrash the 'Nature' shelf, for a few hours at least, before its absence of illustrations revealed its fieldmark of being 'Various Hard to Classify', like that section in the record shop in Austin?

Or perhaps this, the Other Book, belongs in an, as yet to be invented, subsection of 'DIY', showing how a paraquel once journeyed with a Proper Book – a starting point for others who might go that way?

Pages with words on are what makes a book. If it does not have a label by which it can be marketed, then that will make it an unmarketed-book, but it will not stop it being a book, I told myself as I rounded my next corner and stopped to watch a wren busy herself on the top of a hedge. Then she disappeared down into the denser growth of last year, more at home in her Latin name of *troglodytes troglodytes*.

When I checked my bird book for the correct spelling of *troglodytes* it opined of the wren, 'tiny, plump, extremely active and pugnacious'. Tiny and active did accord with the energetic going about their errands that I associated with wrens, but never having argued over an insect with a wren I would have to take pugnacious on trust.

Shall I worry about whether I have chosen the wrong hides for my watching? All the exotic, brightly-coloured rarities, that have not been extensively documented, may be somewhere else.

So be it.

'Contentment is Wealth' had said the sculpture's pedestal in Ennis. I am enjoying the setting of the hides I have chosen. I am finding interest in the behaviour of the puddle-drinking sparrows.

I have booked my November travel. I have chosen to look at sheets of paper in libraries up, down and in the middle of New York State. I will sit quietly and see what I see.

~

Some of the leaves I was happy to scuff, when they were away from home, had been rounded up by the wind and were waiting for me to open my front door. Then, uninvited, they blew in, huddling in twos and threes. I was irked, but decided to make the leaves useful. I would treat myself to leaf-sweeping as a writing-break during the next day.

There is a phrase in one of Seamus Heaney's poems 'the way we are living ... will have been our life.' I could choose to be irritated by inblown leaves and ignore them grumpily. Or I could choose to sweep them up to cheerful purpose. That choice too was part of the background of this, my autumn, which will, come what may, have leaves in it.

~

I started my next new day rearranging again some of Iceland's rocks and stones, my nose still smelling the sulphurous water and surprising myself as I found W H Auden in the same swimming pool as me in the far north of the country.

Then I opened a new tab on my laptop to see what was nesting in my email's inbox. Some newsletter readers had responded. Their enjoyment lit up my inbox (and I might even have danced round the kitchen while I waited for the kettle to boil for my second coffee of the morning, but, if I wrote that, I might commit the sin of over-sharing).

'We make a living by what we get, we make a life by what we give' is attributed to Winston Churchill. It is more outward facing than, 'Never get so busy making a living that you forget to make a life', which in turn takes me back to Seamus Heaney, since without a conscious decision to do something else, the making a living will have been a life.

Over the next few days the flock of enquiring emails returned home to my email address, some bearing gifts of new ideas, some with alternative options or updated practicalities.

November was coming.

11

Reading rooms
in November

5 0,000 square miles was one answer while the other answer was 54,000 square miles. I tried both questions again, through different websites, but the answer, give or take some rounding, was the same.

The area of New York State is larger than the area of England. It is stating the obvious to say that New York State is more than New York City, but in the past I had fallen into thinking that New York was the city, the place familiar from its starring role in countless films and TV series, with the boroughs behind it and then a scattering of suburbs and the barest implication of a handful of small towns beyond that.

I tried another comparison, but for reasons best known to those who construct algorithms, typing in EU size brought up a variety of shoe size conversion charts. It was an illustration of embedded assumptions. In that case the assumption was obviously wrong and I knew what I got was not what I was looking for, but what about less obvious assumptions so deeply embedded the layman does not know they are there?

I turned my attention from the abstract to the particular, the question of getting from one end of New York State to the other, via the nearly mid-way point of Ithaca, the town nearest to Cornell's campus. Mousing around the internet I found a bus from midtown New York City to Cornell campus. I booked and moved on to the second leg. The algorithms I encountered disapproved of one-way travel. They insisted. I must go back to my starting point. I inverted my folly and went searching for destinations instead.

The website offered a request stop which would be conveniently close to my hotel in Buffalo, itself close to the campus with the library that was the point of my trip to Buffalo. The request stop would also be away from the variability of city centre traffic and the harsher realities of city centre bus stations. The algorithm sniffed. It might, if I really pushed its buttons, let me travel one-way, but it would not let me buy a ticket to a request stop.

I therefore concluded that booking a bus ticket to Buffalo International Airport was something to be done in person at New York City's Port Authority Bus Terminal.

~

Once I was in the Bus Terminal I had to find the booking office, not something that the signage encouraged. The Terminal was a place designed for those who knew where they were going. I persisted and found myself a queue to stand in. It was not a particularly long queue, but it was a slow one and shuffling along it involved stepping over pools of liquids that no one in the queue wished to identify. I could feel myself using up more than one day's quota of persistence. After 20 minutes I reached the front and discovered I stood between my opposite number and her rest break.

From her position behind the ticket counter she surveyed my request for a one-way ticket, starting in Ithaca and ending at Buffalo's airport.

After some keyboard tapping, she consulted her screen and issued the result, 'It's not on the computer.'

With both the computer and her delayed rest break against me, I risked a further question, 'Does your computer show Buffalo International Airport as a request stop?'

She looked down at me and then again at her computer screen. Despite my delaying her break, she turned back to me, 'Yes. I will find a way. I will do it manually.'

While there was no scripted smile at ten paces and no rehearsed, 'Hello, my name is blank, how are you today, how can I help you', that was real customer service. I had asked an awkward question at an inconvenient time and she had put herself out to answer me. She had taken up the challenge to defeat the algorithm on my behalf.

After some more keyboard work, breaking the journey into two parts, she gave me my two tickets and went off for her break.

~

My next queue was for some Christmas presents for my sister's children. First I had to find the shop on New York City's Fifth Avenue. Then, as I crossed the traffic, I steeled myself for venturing into a foreign place, a shop so trendy that even at the entrance there was a queue of teenagers, waiting to take photos of themselves in front of the doorway display.

Once inside I remembered I had meant to bring from my hotel the small windup torch I keep for dark places I do not know well. Here the assistants were well-drilled. Every ten paces they said hello to their target audience. I ventured to disturb a shirtfolder to ask where I might find the Tshirts I had been asked for. From what I could make out, against the drumming thumps that passed for the store's musical soundtrack, the shirtfolder needed to see a picture before he could help me. In that quarterlight I doubted either of us could see anything much, but he suggested it would be upstairs or downstairs. Where exactly items were to be found appeared to depend on the colour of the item concerned.

I found what seemed most nearly like the requested items and took them to a spotlight so I could check the size labels. Then I joined another short and slow queue. This one had a velvet rope and the floor was not sticky, but it still used up the patience of all of us waiting for another till point to be opened. In front of me a father was saying much of what I was thinking. Why did they have so few tills open? What must their profit margins be when you look at their prices and where the clothes are made? His wife did not disagree that the place was too dark and the music was not what we would call music and the stairs were confusing without any floor numbers and yet, she said, loudly enough for him, and therefore the rest of us, to hear, the boys will be so pleased with these presents.

When it came to my turn (at the till point that was open) the script said, 'Did you find what you were looking for?'

I considered answering truthfully, 'No, but your business model appears predicated on that assumption.' The drumming thumps were loud enough I could have quoted some Louis MacNeice to the scriptspeaker as my reply and she would have nodded, without hearing a word, and moved on to deliver her next line.

Instead I took the conventional wimp-out and said, 'Yes.'

~

The convention at the Butler Library in Columbia University was that students had backpacks. In compliance with this convention the lockers outside the Rare Book & Manuscript Library were tall and thin. My well-travelled sidekick, my bag that was not my suitcase, was short and squat and was reluctant to comply with this local convention. A checked shirt whose bag was also not designed with those lockers in mind, commiserated with me about the unforgiving locker sizes and asked if I was German. I was sorry to disappoint him. (I wondered what loneliness hung behind his statement that he had been hoping this year to meet someone from his region.) I said I was English and in the US only for two weeks, not two semesters. We agreed we were fellow Europeans, so in one sense from the same region. We went our separate ways, taking advantage of the opportunities the US offered us.

I had come to this point after a couple of wrong turnings from the subway exit for the 1 train, my local replacement for the Northern Line while I was in New York City. Suddenly, despite my wrong turnings, there was the large rectangle of the campus of Columbia University, overseen by the Butler Library itself. Larger than any Cambridge court or Oxford quad, the open space did more than cover several city blocks; it transcended them, being apart from the streets of New York that happened to be around it. Here the weight of learning was made manifest in stone and the buildings had no doubt. Pediments and porticos of supreme confidence took their rightful place in the world. The Butler Library declaimed in stone across its entrance, 'Homer, Herodotus, Sophocles, Plato, Aristotle, Demosthenes, Cicero, Virgil'. Having got used to the entry to American buildings being on the first floor, I should not have been surprised to find that entry to the Butler Library fast-tracked me straight onto the second floor.

I presented my credentials, such as they were: my passport and the email confirming that my research account had been opened with the Rare Book & Manuscript Library. In exchange I was given some pieces of paper to show the security guard on the main library gate and the person on reception at the Rare Book & Manuscript Library. As I put my passport away, I pondered. It said I was a British citizen, but somehow we were all trained on entry into the US that our passport was a UK passport and that for the purposes of their American form UK was our nationality, not British.

British can however still be an adjective used to describe the weather, that way we can sidestep the embarrassment of the preceding 'Great' and embrace greatness, with the comfort blanket of deprecating irony.

The weather in early November in New York City was not unrelated to great British weather: damp and grey. I, however, was inside a windowless reading room. I was in the world of

Research. The weather outside was not my concern.

There did come however a time when I decided to declare lunch. I ventured to the outside of the shop that the person on reception had suggested for a swift and local lunch, but I got no further than the entrance.

I wimped out, again. The suggested shop was a deli with a number of different stations in front of which lined up a range of people who knew exactly what they wanted. If any of their first choices had been exhausted they would have known what substitutes would be acceptable, down beyond the fourth and fifth amendment. I would have been hard-pressed even to name the type of bread on their sandwich. I slunk away in search of a place with a menu where I could read the options slowly, get translations and not hold up anyone else's lunchtime.

I found a suitable cafe and with it the opportunity to eavesdrop on a waiter being trained up, by his elder giving him a running commentary on what to look for in customers.

There was something beguiling about coming back to the place called Research. The rhythms I found in April in Austin came back to me within an hour in Columbia. Going to Research was like a geographical place. I had scoped out what I might find there. Before I could enter the place itself I had to produce a passport to identify myself and, at Columbia and the other places of Research, at the threshold of crossing over, I had to fill in some paperwork about my name and address and purpose of visit, much like any other border control place. Once inside each of the places called Research there were regulations about what could be done where, which were broadly similar from place to place, with some local variations to be observed.

I was used to the practicalities of no cases in the reading room: no laptop case, no pencil case and no camera case. Columbia's local variation was suddenly of relevance to me, no glasses case. A few days before setting off to New York City I had taken collection of my first pair of reading glasses. My litany on going out, my personal checklist of keys and purse (and suitable weather protection) did not yet have glasses inserted by rote. I had to take a very conscious decision as to where I took my glasses and, when I left a place I had taken them, I had to take another conscious decision to bring them back. Without their bright silver case they were pieces of inconspicuous plastic, at risk of being trodden on while I persuaded my bag in and out of the locker, so, despite my optician friend's words about the scratching risk, I opted to hang my new glasses on a cord around my neck.

My expectation before I entered was that Research was a solitary and austere place: a box of papers and a reader. And so it was, but I also discovered that Research can be a place of excitement. At the start of each day there was no knowing what the day might bring. The very next sheet of paper might introduce me to a new place to look, a place where perhaps no one else had been before, or at least those who had travelled that way had not been looking in the way I was looking. I might come to the same summit of a conclusion that everyone else did who passed that way, but I might get there by another route. More likely I would come to the same conclusion by the same route, but the view from the top of a hill would be no less enjoyable just because others had seen it too.

Or page after page might yield nothing and the nothing itself might become hypnotic; a routine habit of physically being in the specified place for the allotted hours. That took me back to my days of being a student, revising for exams amid the dangers of staring at a page as a whole, without tasting a morsel of additional information, not even seeing the black words, recumbent, inert and uncaring on the flat page.

The last page of the last folder in the last box was in front of me. I realised I had turned the last page of the documents in Columbia that I had come to see. Had I overlooked some nuance? Certainly. Were the notes I had taken, even from what I had not overlooked, sufficient? Quite possibly not, but I had the freedom of not being an academic, not being comprehensive. I had the luxury of selection, which was also the discipline of being on a tight budget of time. I had noted what on a couple of days in late autumn had seemed of interest. On different days, or to another person, other things would have seemed of interest. So be it. It was unexpectedly early afternoon. The sun was shining and there were some leaves to scuff on my walk south along Riverside Drive, to where I was staying in Upper West Side.

~

Sarah Lawrence College was a train ride from New York City to Bronxville and then a shared taxi ride past the detached houses on the outskirts of Bronxville. There were no British pavements here. What I thought of as gardens came straight out on to the road. Pedestrians were a peculiarity of New York City. Here the car was the ruler once more. The unfenced American yards gave way to the tree-filled parkland of the college's campus, in shades of yellow, orange and red. There was not the sharp demarcation there had been from urban New York City to the academia of Columbia and here the college buildings were ancillary, tucked in behind the trees.

Sarah Lawrence College had been founded in 1926 to educate women 'without reference to the analogy of colleges for men' and by 1954, when MacNeice went there as a visiting lecturer, the college was struggling with the problems of having fees which were the highest in the country and of not having an endowment (so it could not carry a deficit as some of its older neighbours could).

I had not appreciated, until I started turning the pages of the minutes of various sub-committee meetings of the college in 1954, quite how different the label 'liberal arts' made a degree. I came from a country where a degree course is almost invariably a course in one (or perhaps two) specific subjects. For me the concept of a degree includes having a set syllabus and some limited alternatives within it. Under the label 'liberal arts', I found students picking and choosing courses from a smorgasbord of the current faculty members' interests to construct what at the end would label them as 'college-educated'. Within the word 'degree' I had a set of embedded assumptions that I did not even realise were assumptions, inapplicable to where I was sitting, in an unstructured world of opportunity, a land of personalised learning, not meeting the set requirements of the collective body, but developing as an individual.

Perhaps that was why there seemed to be so much smoking on

campus? Focusing on the Individual in the Now?

The archivists of Sarah Lawrence College had also looked out some photographs from the 1950s, groups posed around a piano or arrayed across several sofas. There was plenty of smoking there too. In a group of four girls, three would be smoking (and two wearing silk scarves, tied with befitting style). There were classroom scenes, with teacher and students seated at a self-consciously round table, not in the traditional lecture hall of Lecturer and Taught. No wonder they had such high fees, with a student to faculty ratio of less than seven to one.

I had been reading about the notion that the college was to develop in its students intellectual interests that would continue to be an 'animating principle' throughout their life and the idea of valuing leisure and using it profitably. So far, so individual, but then came the idea of community and learning to live so that each person contributed to the whole. That brought the collective back into the picture. It was one thing to be an individual leader, out front, being a figurehead for a narrative; hard to do, but easy to understand. More rarely articulated was the college President's goal in the 1950s that their students should also be 'skilful in rendering intelligent support to the effective leadership of others'.

~

One of the Sarah Lawrence archivists gave me a lift down to the station at the end of my day in their reading room. I found myself thinking of the German checked shirt in Columbia and feeling very foreign as I observed the start of the event that is Halloween in the US. On the station platform with me were a scattering of ghosts and witches, but on the way to the station I had also seen a giraffe. Once on the train there were two variations of Sherlock Holmes and a beige, but irrepressibly frilly, tutu on a rather exposed ballet dancer, with a slightly more warmly-dressed companion whom I suspected of being a cartoon character I had not grown up with.

The first sight to greet me at New York's Grand Central Station was an enthusiastic team of skeletons, beginning the execution of their plan for the evening.

A pirate, in short shorts and suspended fishnet stockings, was stabbing her smartphone with the same hand that held her plastic cutlass, putting herself, and any passersby who came injudiciously close, at risk of injury. She was not in agreement with the nearby busker playing, 'I am on top of the world.'

I retreated to my hotel's cocoon to review my day's notes.

~

A friend had caught a different train to New York City and we had a weekend of visiting intransitively. It was a discovery of American English for me, the idea of visiting intransitively, without a direct object and thereby having a slightly different meaning, more informal and conversational, with perhaps coffee on the side, than visiting transitively, as you would a castle or a great-aunt.

We did some visiting of specified places, such as The Cloisters Museum, the far northern outpost of the Metropolitan Museum, and walking along the High Line, the freight railway line for the former meatpacking district now converted to an urban park and buzzing with tourists and insects, all taking the last drops of nectar before winter. Going to see *Macbeth* at the Lincoln Center might not count as the conventional 'seeing a show' expected of New York City, but it sat in balanced contrast with the mellow waves of a chamber music concert preceding it.

For me, it was time away from being an Independent Researcher, time away from being solitary, reading and writing alone and thinking in self-containment, but when I took the Staten Island Ferry for the free round trip of classic Manhattan views, I drifted off into thinking how MacNeice would have seen the Statue of Liberty, arriving first in New York City by sea in 1939.

There was a display in the lower Manhattan branch of the Smithsonian American Indian Museum of some collages of driftwood by George Morrison, an Indian whom the blurb told me had at one point been thought not to produce sufficiently Indian works of art, and that set me off thinking about what made a poet Irish or not and wondering some more about the driftwood of the somewhat random assemblage of books that had once been Louis MacNeice's and were now in Columbia's collections.

We took a discursive route to the still-flowering roses in Brooklyn's Botanic Garden, via East Village and the address where W H Auden lived in the 1950s and where I therefore assumed MacNeice would have visited when he was lecturing at Sarah Lawrence College. That address in St Mark's Place felt like an enclave, not tied to the world of timetables by a convenient subway stop and not much concerned with clocks.

That November weekend had been the weekend of the New York marathon and by Monday morning there were still plenty of tracksuits wearing their medals and wondering what to do next. I, too, was beginning to wonder about life after the Proper Book, but I banished such whisperings, with a version of 'put up or shut up'. I either put the whisper into specific form on a numbered list (a list that grows, quietly waiting for its turn in my diary) or the more nebulous 'what about' whisper I shut out, by concentrating on a specific task of now. There was still travel to Cornell and to Buffalo. There was the writing up of what I found there and then there was going into the new world of production, of turning the words in my laptop into a coloured spine that people I would never meet could take down from a shelf.

~

My immediate task was to recline from New York City to the Cornell campus, in a leather seat, passing five hours of varied scenery in a bubble of wi-fi, polysyllables all around me. This was bus travel, but not as I had known it before. There was so much space I had to undo my seat belt and get out of my seat if I wanted to reach the pull-down table in front of me.

We left at lunchtime and New York State steadily became less and less like New York City. At regular intervals a signpost repeated variations on the mantra 'the bridge ices before the road'. The tree branches became barer. Ghostly silver birches faded into the shrinking afternoon. A sign pointed the way to 'Land of Make Believe', presumably a seasonal tourist attraction. The density of carved pumpkins on doorsteps, presided over by US flags, increased as the towns we passed through became smaller and what shops I saw were no longer emblazoned with brandnames

I recognised. The world outside the tinted glass of the bus was subdued, farmland and woodland and land that was just being. My seat neighbour had dozed off part way through reviewing an article on malaria in northern Ghana.

Another road sign, 'It can wait. Text stop 5 miles'.

And then it was dusk and my suitcase and I were out in the fresh air once again. This was bracingly fresh air. It was a scouring wind, as the wind off Belfast Lough had been when I had first ventured out towards the harbour wall at Carrickfergus. This was early November in upstate New York. It was not snowing, but that time was in the air.

I held on tightly to my flapping paper of directions to Telluride House, the location of my bed for the next two nights. I was to bear right and walk downhill, which I could do in the dusk, looking for an orange building behind a clump of trees, which was less easy in the dying evening light. Telluride House was set up in 1910 by a wealthy engineer (L L Nunn) to house about 25 students and two or three faculty members. It had three central goals: intellectual engagement; self-government; and community living. All of which were interesting details but they did not help me locate an orange building when the colour had gone from the day.

I saw some parking spaces behind a clump of trees, so I turned from the main road to see whether they gave any help. Happily they declared themselves to be spaces reserved for Telluride House, so I hunted for a door in the building behind the parking spaces. The first door I tried was open so I went in, armed with the names of my email correspondents and trying not to dwell on the improbability of a Brit coming to stay in a student house just because a long-dead poet had lived there for a few months over 70 years ago. Not only that, but I had graduated from university before most of the student residents were born.

Improbability was no bar to a cheerful welcome. Indeed my taking a year out of corporate life to write a book was, some said, 'so cool', and others even went so far as to call it 'awesome'. I was not sure about either adjective. Both were more trendy than me. 'Mildly improbable' perhaps? Certainly I would put my hand up to 'disciplined and organised', but neither of those are exactly energetic with aspiration.

My time travelling with Louis MacNeice had certainly taken me to places I would not have gone on my own: that thought struck me again as I stood in front of the linen cupboard at Telluride House. The immediate question facing me was whether to take (in addition to the customary sheets and pillowcase to make up my bed) an extra sheet to hang over the window of the room I was staying in. I decided that was an unnecessary refinement, not only was my window not overlooked, sunrise by that time in November was an eminently civilised 7am.

Two single beds, two chairs, two desks, two (full) wastepaper bins and one lightbulb compromised my room's furniture. (The room had been cleared to the standard for a visiting elder sibling, rather than for a parental inspection.)

I had packed my suitcase on the presumption that, as had been the case in Iceland, the bathrooms were likely to be down the hallway, if not down the stairs. Instead, while the room proffered me did not have a curtain on the window, it did have a bathroom attached. That was not a luxury I had as a student and would certainly have been supremely luxurious in 1940 when MacNeice visited. There were built-in wooden cupboards in the bathroom. The receding tide of successive visitors had left flotsam of nearly-finished tubes of toothpaste and other leavings from their washbags on each shelf. There was also a textbook left behind (about aspects of the subconscious) and a three-month old magazine (*The London Review of Books)* plus a large grey ball (of the size to do gym exercises with).

Of Telluride House's three goals I chiefly benefited from the central aspect of community living, namely eating together. Three times a day the residents came together to eat at long wooden tables in their dining room, beyond which were a pool table, a table tennis table and a table football table.

These free meals were not school dinners of cut-price stodge, but varied (even exotic) combinations: Vietnamese soup, meat and veg-filled rolls, rounded off with a banana pudding for my first Telluride meal.

As in 1940, so in 2013 there were about 25 student residents (undergraduates and postgraduates) and faculty members. In the dining room they started or resumed conservations with whoever they happened to sit next to. It was the differences between Remembrance Day in the UK and Veterans Day in the US that accompanied the first course. There were two other visitors from England that evening so we did not notice when someone, whose native English was Indian English, used the word *Fortnight.* Another European English speaker spotted it, a non-American word deriving from a truncated fourteen nights. Is it when tired, or perhaps just relaxed, that we revert, unfiltered, to the familiars of our childhood language? At what point does a non-native speaker stop translating in their head? 'What time do you make it?' was a simple question or a nonsensical fabrication, depending on whether it was asked of an Old World or a New World English listener. The conversation splintered off from there and by the banana pudding there was the extent to which tourist merchandise strengthened or weakened the economy of the visited area to consider.

I wondered about the dynamics of debate, of building a common experience while coming from, and going to, different worlds beyond Cornell. In term-time the pull back from any part of campus to Telluride for lunch and dinner would be strong: why pay money for what is free back at the house? Day in and day out the goal of community living would not be something to be thought of consciously, but Cook Susan provided the starting point, it seemed to me, from which all other aspects of being a community were built.

One weekday evening a week there would be a housemeeting when the residents put into action the goal of self-government: sitting down to discuss, and decide on, such things as the redecoration schedule for the house both inside and out, the sourcing of lightbulbs or the censure for those infringing what had been agreed collectively.

My time in the house did not coincide with a housemeeting, but I was there for a 'pubspeak'. In active pursuit of the goal of intellectual engagement, each resident had an obligation to give an hour's presentation to their fellow housemembers on a topic of 'personal intellectual interest'. Until that evening I did not even know I was ignorant of 1920s constructivism in architecture, which was the topic for that week's pubspeak.

Comfortably lodged in the corner of a more than three-seater sofa, I started further behind the rest of the audience, not having heard the speaker enthuse on matters architectural over several months of mealtimes and being without any architectural framework into which I could put the architecture of the 1920s. (I did, just about, have a rudimentary structure of European history of the 1920s, into which I could try to insert some architecture.) Having such presentations was also about making connections the listener and the speaker would not otherwise make, for as well as the obligation on each housemember to give a presentation, there was the reciprocal obligation to listen to others' presentations and ask questions about them.

Yes, there was factual knowledge imparted too. It was received and held by those who had a place to hang such knowledge. For me, and any like me who had no pre-existing place to hang the new information, the pubspeak was a place for new ideas to trip over old ones and so find something else in the ensuing tangle.

It was the social corridor I remembered: the corridor that led to the new style, constructivist, flats, the corridor that might be a meeting place itself, rather than just the way to the front door, but only if there was a reason (or at least an excuse) to loiter in the corridor longer than the time it took to walk through an individual's front door.

Putting individuals in the same building did not make them a community.

Telluride House had plenty of corridors and cushioned benches under windows or in hallways, but it was the dining room that seemed the more social space, a place entered for a reason and then, at a time of the diner's choosing, left.

It was a luxury, not to rush on to the next task but to loiter, whether in a theoretical constructivist corridor or while sitting over an actual breakfast discussing Irish involvement in the second world war or the 1940s layout of Cornell campus. It was another case of visiting intransitively (now I knew about the American sense of such visiting).

Not having any obligations; no time to be at a specified place at any time all day, was a type of freedom, one that I could appreciate because it was not permanent. No obligation brought no responsibility, but also no belonging and no community. There was no-one to notice my absence or presence.

With the sunrise Telluride House did assume its trademark orange colour. The chimes from Cornell's McGraw Tower that had woken both MacNeice and me at 7.45am are played three times a day by those admitted as chimesmasters, people who must be able to manage the 161 steps to the top of the tower, as well as be able to read sheet music.

I opted for the easier route to a view over the campus, by going to the fifth floor of the Herbert F Johnson Museum of Art. (Cornell, like the other US universities I visited, had a name for everything, usually with a middle initial too.) In amongst the exhibits were a series of blue lights, lined up in strips with a white background. They were there to catch flies, not to be admired as an art installation, but that set me off thinking about what was, or was not, within the definition of art and who made and remade that definition. That led me on to what was a definition of success and who made that definition. One of the notices I had read on one of the Telluride noticeboards had been a purpose statement from the most recent overseeing convocation of the Telluride Association, which had included an emphasis on the role and value of failure, the importance of feeling the impact of things not going to plan and thereby learning how to move out from under that disappointment to somewhere better.

When I first left the house after breakfast there was still some warmth in the sun. On the stone paving slab of my first walkway there was a shuffling orange and black caterpillar, scrunching itself up and then expanding again to inch along. I stood and watched, just because I could. I was outside, in the daylight, doing the equivalent of smelling the roses.

Then the sky clouded over and the wind sharpened; the relevance (at the top of the grassy slope below the Arts Quad) of the signs saying, 'No skiing', became more obvious.

By the time I returned home to the house the prickled outlines of manically-dancing branches were shadowing my bedroom wall. There was no curtain to shut them out.

It was a rough night. I commiserated with the taxi driver who took me down the hill from Cornell campus to Ithaca bus terminal.

My onward bus was more like bus travel as I have known it, but it was still clean and with washed windows waiting for daydreams.

I was not sure what reply to give when the bus driver, counting heads before we set off, said somewhat gruffly, 'See someone has told you about my driving.' He nodded towards my body, 'Wearing a seatbelt.' Having already put myself in an unpopular category of one by having the temerity to ask to be dropped at my booked request stop and knowing seatbelts are not a legal requirement in various states of the US, in my best English accent I backtracked from any implied slight on his manly driving prowess, 'It's just a habit from home.' To my surprised relief he cheered up, 'It's a good habit. Don't see it often.'

I opted for country music playing in my ears as we set off westwards, past a road named 'Deerlick spur', then a scattering of houses between harvested fields of brown stalks. Some of the houses marked their boundaries with faded children's toys, their once-primary colours drained. A town called Romulus; a village called Ovid, Seneca County; all disconcertingly Classical and then a lakeside stop was announced, 'Geneva, New York', which was as it should be for my fellow passengers, but sounded a strange hybrid to me.

People got off and continued their stories with those who were expecting them.

Earlier in the autumn, driving myself around Connemara in a rental car I had partially insulated myself from Ireland in a bubble of wheeled independence. That way I had been able to get done what I had wanted to in a shorter time, but now I was back on public transport, amid the interlacings of other people's lives.

The remainder of the bus continued west, to Rochester, a more-battered place, where the rain came down harder.

A skein of geese flew south. There was a sign to Corfu, but our next stop was by a filling station, pausing on a piece of land lumpy with water-filled potholes. There was no doubting we were in a northern November where the living was not easy.

Inside the bus a sign pronounced that federal law prohibited the operation of the bus while someone was standing forward of the white line. What if there was not a white line and therefore nowhere for us all to be behind? Could the bus operate at all if it could not be proved that none of us were in front of the white line we could not see?

Taking pleasure in simpler things there was a toddler in the seats in front of me who had been moving an empty juice carton from the drinks-holder space by her father to the drinks-holder space by her mother, to her evident satisfaction, until, all of a sudden, she decided neither place was right any more. Her father swiftly forestalled her disappointed tears with a distracting and empty cardboard packet, the size of a playing card, that she could look into, put her fingers into and then, to great beams of joy that had to be shared, even with the foreigner in the seat behind her family, she found that the packet could be opened and shut and opened again.

And then it was time for me to leave another story part-written, to move onto the next section of my MacNeice travelling, beginning at my last place of Research, the State University of New York at Buffalo.

~

When I had walked round the ten open gardens in the historic Fourth District area of Charlotte when the year was a young April, one gardener had downplayed the road noise, it was her urban ocean. My hotel room at the edge of the north campus of the University at Buffalo was also by an urban ocean, but being a constant noise, it was soothing, like the ocean, a place of reflection, a boundary place between Research, where I felt now nearly at home, and the unplanned horizon of what next, beyond January's practicalities of production.

Walking in New York City was a normal activity; walking in Bronxville had been, at best, possible; but walking, at least by my urban ocean in Buffalo, was not what people did. I picked out an off-road route, worn by the subversives who had gone before me, to a service road that lead on to the campus. The buildings of the University at Buffalo had none of the confidence of Columbia's, nor was the campus tree-softened as the campus for Sarah Lawrence College had been. I had heard that the 1970s built, out of town, north campus was designed in reaction to the 1960s student unrest in many universities, including Buffalo. It seemed a featureless place of red brick, defined by encircling multi-lane highways. The only gathering spaces seemed to be those for cars. The only human touch was a VW Beetle with long, flirtatious, black plastic eyelashes fixed to the top and bottom of its headlights. Buffalo's campus did have the wind in common with Cornell's, but this late in the first semester its bookshop had a sign recommending potential customers ask a member of staff if they had a question about books – there were not many books to be seen on the shop's shelves.

I found an entrance to the Silverman Library, but the elevator from the signed white buffalo eluded me.

I looked again at my directions. Definitely it was a white

buffalo I was looking for, a white buffalo that had been signed.

I could not see any white buffalo, signed or unsigned.

Now I was inside the red brick building, the temperature seemed unseasonably warm. Down with my waterproof's hood and off with my fleece hat. Here, after barren tarmac and bland concrete, were people. I could hear their assorted languages, some spoken urgently, some mockingly and some in patient explanation.

I tried again to relate the directions I had been sent with where I found myself.

I began to wonder if Buffalo was indeed the answer to my asking the wrong question.

12

And so to print

It could not be commanded, nor could it be anticipated.

It was there, for a moment, just as we were leaving.

A friend had driven out of her way to take me to see Niagara Falls and there in the waterfall's spray, as we stood in the US looking out across to Canada, was a rainbow.

In the Icelandic summer, outside Keflavik airport, there had been a rainbow sculpture, permanent with the promise of possibilities and of future sun meeting passing rain.

In May on the north Atlantic there had been a double rainbow, overarching the containership and shown to me by one of the officers.

Now, as my MacNeice voyage drew to its shore, here was another rainbow. It was an apt metaphor for my writing year: some things I could make a detailed plan for and others just happened.

What of the waterfalls of Niagara itself? Well I did feel sorry for the American Falls. If they had not been so close to the main event, the Horseshoe Falls, they would have been feted as dramatically impressive in their own right. Instead they were swept into the umbrella term of Niagara Falls and taken in by a backward glance when visitors had exhausted every other angle of the Horseshoe Falls.

Large volume of water? Tick.

From a height? Tick.

Thunderingly loud with a dense spray misting its surroundings? Tick, tick. Indeed the spray had been rising like smoke from fires for several miles of our approach.

How about the setting? Yes Niagara Falls got the bonus points for waterfalls that are photogenic for ordinary people with ordinary cameras, though it would also be dramatic when seen with specialist equipment overhead. Standing on the pavement in Canada looking at the US gave more panoramic, sweeping views than those to be seen when in the US looking at Canada, but from neither country were the waterfalls exactly pretty. They were powerful, choosing for the time being to be contained within defined boundaries. They were open to all (though the cost of car parking on both sides was enough to make Iceland seem like better value than it had at the time). The waterfalls were just there, at the edge of the firm world, with a flat pavement running (or walking, with lots of stops for photographs) along the edge of the river.

And then, for me, there was a rainbow on an otherwise ordinarily cold and damp morning.

It was, I think, Freya Stark, the travel writer made Dame Commander of the Order of the British Empire in 1972, for whom the title doyenne seemed most fitting, who opined, 'One should never have a fixed time for arriving.'

I did agree that not having an eye on a deadline gave two eyes for the wider world. Rushing for a set time increased the likelihood of body-swerving a lamppost or otherwise pumping up the heart-rate while grazing against a mundane practicality. When I was not listening to my inner tour guide, worrying about the next departing connection, I had both ears free to eavesdrop.

Flexibility in arrival time might also lead to arriving early.

I had set myself nine months for the travelling and the writing and then, so I had written on my plan, it would be January, time to put my head down and to sharpen my pencils, the time for editing and working my way through the production phase of the 12 chapters of the Proper Book and of this, the Other Book. On that basis, arrival would be at the end of December.

Instead it was mid-November, an unadvertised Saturday morning in the US. I had, unexpectedly, arrived at my paraquel's closing chapter.

After seeing Niagara Falls from both sides and answering two sets of border questions, we had lunch (not of that strange hybrid called buffalo chicken wings that I had first met on the north Atlantic) swopping stories, before driving around some of the past still visible in Buffalo, where, despite the single-digit Fahrenheit winters, rocking chairs and swinging seats hung outside, waiting in companionable silence to be warmed by returning summer.

All the while the morning's metaphor was gently, but insistently, reminding me that this was the closing chapter, at least for this, the Other Book.

～

Once I had located the white buffalo and the elevators behind it, I had, two days before Niagara's rainbow, left behind the doubtfulness of Buffalo and found myself again in my favourite place of my writing year. I was in Research. I was immersed, beyond the units of minutes and hours. I was an outsider who had been let in to feast on the riches waiting within the vanilla folders of Buffalo's Poetry Collection.

For me, the exercise book of MacNeice's notes made in Iceland brought Buffalo out from the shadow of its later 20th century decline and into the visionary light of those in the 1930s who had built up The Poetry Collection, asking poets, who might be famous in the future, for their notebooks to be sent to Buffalo, instead of being thrown away.

On New York City's Staten Island ferry there had been a poster for the ferry company, 'Life is short, enjoy the ride.' It was a free ride, like scuffing leaves or catching sight of an unscheduled rainbow or turning over a page of manuscript and reading words that went straight from the page to inside my ear. I savoured again reading MacNeice writing about where we had both been.

Turning over the final pages of the exercise book in Buffalo I knew also there was a sadness, as well as a resilience, when the Sufi poets said, 'This too shall pass.'

~

The cover of MacNeice's autobiography says 'unfinished autobiography', which, in a sense, all autobiographies are. In his case the draft chapters were put into book form after his death by his literary executor, so MacNeice had done less finishing of that book than of his other published works.

I was planning to have printed a book about writing a book, which provided a chicken and egg conundrum of when could that book be finished. How to write about the production of a book that could not be produced if I was still adding to the text of the book by writing about its production? That way lies the unfinished project in search of unattainable completeness.

'My book, my rules'. I decided to add an appendix, like the text that comes up at the end of a film, about events that happened after filming was completed.

~

One of the poems at the back of *Letters from Iceland* was written by MacNeice and Auden together. It was called *Last Will and Testament*. It derived, so I imagined, from them talking, while waiting for their homeward-bound transport, about those they had not seen in weeks and what would make them happy or perhaps what they deserved (which is not always the same thing). It was therefore full of people, their friends and family and others they knew. It had lots of names.

I realised that few of the people in either the Proper Book or this, the Other Book, had names. It had seemed something of a liberty to drag people out of the breathing world and affix them onto my page. I had instead sketched a few of those who had shared some MacNeiceing with me, applying a few light phrases, some lines from a past moment.

I have given myself a name, but I too, the author of these pages, am a sketched likeness, perhaps a concentrated essence of part of the person known by my friends and family: a truth, but not the whole truth, and one unfinished.

Or perhaps I am the same as the author, but within a well-cut winter coat of metaphor, which accentuates a certain public appearance. The outlines are mine, but some details are kept, consciously, out of sight. It is the weather for such a coat. If the circumstances had been other, the outer garment would have been other, but it is my coat, cut with the cloth of the nine months I gave myself. It is perhaps a coat that has a sweeping tendency to metaphorical flights of fancy and, left to its own devices, it might twirl in a handful of unqualified generalisations, but it also takes a pride in accomplishing the job designated, the writing of a book.

Writing about writing changes the writing.

It is a truth that sounds like an exam question, 'Discuss the application of Heisenberg's Uncertainty Principle to writing.' The very act of measuring changes the context in which the measurement is being made. I had started this book with the idea of jotting down every fifth day a few lines about that day, or about the four days before it, or perhaps just about the five minutes before, so that gradually over my nine months of writing, layer by layer, I would build up a record of what those nine months were like.

The act of making notes was an act of stopping, reflecting, taking myself out of the flow of actually doing whatever the It of the moment had been. Building up those notes, layer by layer, included, within each layer, an editing to give shape, the shape as it seemed to me as I wrote, which may not be the shape as it seems to others when they read or indeed to me when I am further away from this writing year.

The grey cells were at it again – talking to themselves. To be fair to them, my grey cells, along with my pen and paper, kept me good company, as I unpacked and repacked, totting up my three months on the road, but to keep me from slipping into two dimensions I needed regular time off the road, away from tasks and even from my books, time with those sketched and unsketched. It was time to rejoin myself in south London.

As I checked out of my hotel room in Buffalo there was a dusting of the first snow of winter outside. 'Pretty until Christmas, boring until April,' said the receptionist.

Heading home again to south London, I was standing on a train, in that boundary place before arriving.

'Oh it was all very political. It was only Vladimir who even mentioned Jesus,' a mobile phone told all of us in the carriage. A short story opened up as we slowed down for Clapham Junction and then there was a softer, female voice nearer to me, 'He doesn't use his Portuguese in Sierra Leone.' Would I put her in the same short story? She sounded sad. Had he expected to be using his Portuguese there? Had they learnt it together? Had she taught him? Or had he been away too long, with the previous job and now this one? What was the language they still had in common?

My suitcase, my laptop and I gathered ourselves together. We had our own words to write, the Proper Book and the paraquel which did also veer off, away from the route, just for fun and because it could, because it was interested in, and distracted by, the possible implications of an absence of Portuguese in Sierra Leone.

The advertisement posters on the train station were full of laptops that became tablets and showed split screens. Doing two things at once seemed to be a current fashion, perhaps even trendy.

It was time for me to be in one place, at home, with my own light switches.

Traditionally those returning home talk about coming home to their own beds, but I also miss my own light switches when I am away. At home I know which switch is which, which are on the wall and which are on a cord, and what each turns on. At home in south London I do not have a master switch on a keypad, itself seven or eight steps of darkness away from the entrance door. I do not have a dangling cord behind the ironing board in the wardrobe that turns off the desk light at the other side of the room. Yes, if truth be told, I do have several switches that do not do anything at all, but I have the luxury of knowing about them, in advance.

~

I was typing again in south London.

It was a Thursday lunchtime in later November and I realised I had written the final sentence of the Proper Book.

There was not the finality of typing in bold and upper case THE END. I knew there was plenty more work to be done, but the travelling, the reading around, the mulling over, the filling in of a once blank sheet of planning paper, the capturing, that was now done.

To come was the egg and chicken of requesting permissions to use copyright material and to quote from the papers held in the various libraries I had visited. Until I had written the Proper Book I did not know what I would like to quote. Until I had the permissions to use other people's words I had not finished writing the Proper Book.

To come too was learning about the book production world beyond the world of annual report production that I already knew and with that would come working with others, who, understandably, would see things their way in their own time.

I had set out to Austin in April to write a book. With the aid of strengthening winds on a containership in the north Atlantic, Irish rain on country roads and all the places I would not have gone, but for Louis MacNeice, I now had 100,000 words written in November.

Having spent so many months in such close proximity with my travelling companion, did I still like Louis MacNeice and his poetry?

Yes, at their best his words were direct, with a mixture of the wry and the dark that I still enjoyed. He had the talent and intellectual ability to turn his head to many different tasks; but living with all of him, not just his words and his stories, would have been at times trying and indeed more than trying at many times.

While I had been travelling with Louis MacNeice I had got to know others in the party.

His father too was a talented and intellectually able man, but also difficult at times to live with. His mother was only the faintest of sketches, dying when MacNeice was barely seven, but perhaps giving him some of her intense enjoyment of the moment and also some of her darkest fears beyond the reach of logic or daylight. His sister was an elder sister like me, so it was not surprising that I was glad of her company, balancing some of his childhood recollections. His stepmother, in her 40s, found herself with three stepchildren, two boys being much higher maintenance than the girl, and she took on the job in its entirety.

Then there was the younger Auden, a much more practical and organised chap than I had expected to meet, and there was the wise constancy of Eric Dodds, MacNeice's first employer, who was for the rest of his life a counsellor to MacNeice. When I knew only that Dodds was Irish and Regius Professor of Greek at Oxford, I had begun with a stereotype. Dodds had warned me of the ease of stereotypes and, learning more, I appreciated his other dimensions.

Where were we (MacNeice, his family, his friends and me) travelling to? I privately looked forward to lodging the Proper Book in the required copyright libraries and libraries where future researchers interested in MacNeice would go and perhaps find something deserving of a footnote in their own dissertation, but that was a destination I would never know if I had reached.

More obviously this writing was about bringing the poetry of Louis MacNeice out into the view of some who had not seen it before and of showing poetry to be a part of the mainstream world.

Most of all, travelling with the poetry of Louis MacNeice and into the daylight of not writing a bestseller for nine months had been about taking the first opportunity, which may be the only opportunity (though there might be other opportunities, in brackets, behind the first one).

Some opportunities may sound like a slamming door. They may look like a piece of paper with the wrong grade. They may be an absence and then how much longer to wait? For the next train? For the next postal delivery? For the next year? Or just take the unpromising thing, pass it through a silver-lining generator and call it an opportunity?

Some opportunities are tucked away, barely visible, behind the serried ranks of sensible things to do next. They do not have one of those conference name badges on them saying 'Opportunity'. They have no indication on them of where they are from, nor of how much they might cost.

Carpe diem is a phrase that has crossed over from its native habitat in an ode by Horace to a place of encouragement in nearly-colloquial English usage. It is most often translated as 'Seize the day', but there are softer, gentler translations and MacNeice translated the phrase as 'Gather the day'.

I have gathered a collection of days, of travelling, from further places to nearer places. I have left the unknowable to its own time. I have written and now, warmly wrapped in my winter coat of metaphors, I pass what I have written to you reader.

Appendix of miscellany
and some notes about practicalities

My zig-zag between Daylight and Sunlight.

As I mentioned in chapter 6, while I was waiting for the words I had written in the chapter of one book to settle before I disturbed them by editing, I wrote a chapter or two of the other book. The zig-zag between them went something like this:

Sunlight	Daylight
	1
	2
1	
2	
	3
	4
3	
	5
	6
4	
5	
	7
6	
7	
8	
	8
	9
9	
10	
11	
	10
12	
	11
	12

Hypothetical *Desert Island Disc* choices in the north Atlantic of May 2013:

A list made when the sea in chapter 5 was too rough for typing and inspired by the BBC radio programme *Desert Island Discs*.

	Choices that would be illustrative of different times in my life	Music without (English) words to bear repeated repetition if a castaway
1	*Ultravox* by Vienna	Holst's *Planets*
2	*Born in the USA* by Bruce Springsteen	Poulenc's *Organ Concerto*
3	*Clare Island* by The Saw Doctors	Prokofiev's *Alexander Nevsky*
4	*A Ship called Dignity* by Deacon Blue	J S Bach's organ fugues
5	Recording of Homer's *Odyssey* (translated by Robert Fagles and read by Ian McKellen)	Mozart's *Clarinet Concerto*
6	*Mad World* by Tears for Fears	Sibelius' *Finlandia* (with a boxed set of his symphonies if the BBC would let me have that as one choice)
7	*Back Down South* by Kings of Leon	Schubert's *Trout Quintet*
8	*One day like this* by Elbow	Orff's *Carmina Burana*

Books of reference for production phase
(though I decided to ignore some of what they suggested):

New Hart's Rules, Oxford University Press, 2005

Writers' & Artists' Yearbook 2013, Bloomsbury, 2012

Baverstock, Alison, *Is there a book in you?* A & C Black, 2006

Baverstock, Alison, *The Naked Author: A guide to Self-Publishing,* Bloomsbury, 2011

Blake, Carole, *From Pitch to Publication: Everything You Need to Know to Get Your Novel Published,* Macmillan, 1999

Rooney, Mick, *A Seriously Useful Author's Guide: To Self-Publish or Not to Self-Publish,* Kibworth Beauchamp, Troubador, 2010

How long did it take to write?

In round figures I spent 250 hours typing the first draft of *Daylight* and refining the second draft of 83,000 words and 300 hours doing the same for 103,000 words of *Sunlight*, plus 76 hours in various US libraries making notes for *Sunlight*. (I did not keep track of my planning, thinking or wider reading time.)

And after chapter 12?

Eight people read some or all of the text of one or both of the books as initially typed.

I thought about the comments of those beta readers and worked with others to copy-edit for consistency: 84 hours polishing up *Daylight* and 120 hours polishing up *Sunlight*. In chapter 1 I had thought it would be seven drafts from initial typescript to print-ready proof: *Daylight* was five printed-out drafts and *Sunlight* was eight until I handed the text over to typesetting from where it was another two proofs to print-ready files. I had set myself 12 months to get from blank computer screen to printed book: it took me nearly 15 months, albeit for two books.

In tandem with the polishing, I was getting the necessary permissions in relation to quotations for *Sunlight* and learning more about typography and book production and then partnering with others on page design and layout; jacket design; indexing; drawing a map of Iceland; proofreading; printing and binding; and distribution: another 70 or so hours of my time before I handed over the text of both books for typesetting into the agreed page design.

For *Daylight* there were 48 more hours I spent proofreading and reviewing other proofreaders' comments before I 'passed for press'.

Bibliography

The following is a list of books about MacNeice and about places and ideas associated with my writing year. The place of publication is not given where it is London or where it is part of the publisher's name. The list is of the editions I used – more recent ones may now be available. Some are books I have consulted regularly throughout my writing year; others I read through from front to back and yet others I only dipped into a few times.

Arnheim, Rudolf; Auden, W H; Shapiro, Karl; Stauffer, Donald A (with introduction by Charles D Abbott), *Poets at Work: Essays based on the Modern Poetry collection at the Lockwood Memorial Library, University of Buffalo,* New York, Harcourt, Brace, 1948

Auden, W H, *About the House,* Faber, 1966

Auden, W H, and MacNeice, Louis, *Letters from Iceland,* Faber, 1937

Beckett, J Angus, *Iceland Adventure: the Double Traverse of Vatnajokull by the Cambridge Expedition,* H F & G Witherby, 1934

Booker, Christopher, *The Seven Basic Plots: Why we tell stories,* continuum, 2004

Boyes, Roger, *Meltdown Iceland: How the Global Financial Crisis Bankrupted an Entire Country,* Bloomsbury, 2009

Brearton, Fran, and Longley, Edna (eds.), *Incorrigibly Plural: Louis MacNeice and His Legacy,* Manchester, Carcanet, 2012

Brown, Terence, *Northern Voices: Poets from Ulster,* Dublin, Gill and Macmillan, 1975

Brown, Terence and Reid, Alec (eds.), *Time Was Away: the World of Louis MacNeice,* Dublin, Dolmen Press, 1975

Cook, Thomas, *The Traveller's Handbook for Norway, Sweden and Denmark including Spitsbergen, Iceland and other Arctic Islands,* Thomas Cook, 1923

Coulton, Barbara, *Louis MacNeice in the BBC,* Faber, 1980

Dasent, Sir George Webbe, *The Story of Burnt Njal,* Dent Dutton, 1971

Dodds, E R, *Missing Persons: An Autobiography,* Oxford University Press, 1977

Evans, Andrew, *Iceland: the Bradt Travel Guide,* Chalfont St Peter, Bradt, 2011

Fitzpatrick, David, *'Solitary and Wild': Frederick MacNeice and the Salvation of Ireland,* Dublin, Lilliput, 2012

Follett, Mary Parker, *Prophet of Management: A Celebration of Writings from the 1920s,* (ed. Pauline Graham, preface by Rosabeth Moss Kanter, introduction by Peter F Drucker), Cambridge, Mass., Harvard Business School, 1995

Gielgud, Val, *British Radio Drama, 1922–1956: a Survey,* Harrap, 1957

Heuser, Alan (ed.), *Selected Prose of Louis MacNeice,* Oxford University Press, 1990

Juvenal, *Sixteen Satires Upon the Ancient Harlot,* (trans. Steven Robinson), Manchester, Carcanet, 1983

Levinson, Marc, *The Box: How the Shipping Container Made the World Smaller and the World Economy Bigger,* Princeton University Press, 2006

MacNeice, Louis, *Collected Poems,* (ed. E R Dodds), Faber, 1979 (first published in 1966)

MacNeice, Louis, *I Crossed the Minch,* Edinburgh, Polygon, 2007 (first published by Longman in 1938)

MacNeice, Louis, *Letters of Louis MacNeice,* (ed. Jonathan Allison), Faber, 2010

MacNeice, Louis, *Louis MacNeice: Poems,* (ed. Michael Longley), Faber, 2001

MacNeice, Louis, *Out of the Picture: a play in two acts,* Faber, 1937

MacNeice, Louis, *Persons from Porlock and other plays for radio,* British Broadcasting Corporation, 1969

MacNeice, Louis (writing as Louis Malone), *Roundabout Way,* Capuchin Classics, 2012 (first published in 1932)

MacNeice, Louis, *Selected Poems,* (ed. W H Auden), Faber, 1964

MacNeice, Louis, (trans.) *The Agamemnon of Aeschylus,* Faber, 1967 (first published in 1936)

MacNeice, Louis, *The Dark Tower,* Faber, 1964 (first published in 1947)

MacNeice, Louis, *The Dark Tower and Other Radio Scripts,* Faber, 2008 (first published in 1947)

MacNeice, Louis, *The Mad Islands and The Administrator: two radio plays,* Faber, 1964

MacNeice, Louis, *The Strings are False: an Unfinished Autobiography,* (ed. E R Dodds), Faber, 1982 (first published in 1965)

MacNeice, Louis, *Varieties of Parable,* Faber, 2008

Magnusson, Sally, *Dreaming of Iceland: The lure of a family legend,* Hodder & Stoughton, 2004

Marsack, Robyn, *The Cave of Making: The Poetry of Louis MacNeice,* Oxford University Press, 1982

Moore, D B, *The Poetry of Louis MacNeice,* Leicester University Press, 1972

O'Neill, Michael; and Reeves, Gareth, *Auden, MacNeice, Spender: The Thirties Poetry,* Basingstoke, Macmillan Education, 1992

Peterson, Roger Tory; Mountfort, Guy; and Hollom, P A D, *Collins Field Guide Birds of Britain & Europe,* HarperCollins, 1993

Press, John, *Louis MacNeice: Writers & their Work 187,* Harlow, Longman, 1970

Ramsden, D M, *Tramping through Iceland,* Liverpool, Henry Young & Sons, 1931

Robinson, Tim, *Connemara: The Last Pool of Darkness,* Penguin, 2009

Royal Geographical Society, *Hints to Travellers: Eleventh Edition, Volume Two,* Edited by the secretary with the help of many travellers, Royal Geographical Society, 1938

Smith, P R (ed.), *On The Air: five Radio and Television Plays,* Sydney, Angus & Robertson, 1959

Soames, Mary (ed.), *Speaking for Themselves: the Personal Letters of Winston and Clementine Churchill,* Black Swan, 1999

Spender, Stephen (ed.), *W H Auden – A tribute,* Weidenfeld & Nicolson, 1975

Stallworthy, Jon, *Louis MacNeice,* Faber, 1995

Stefansson, Stefan, *Iceland: Handbook for Tourists,* Reykjavik, Hekla Travel Bureau, 1930

Stoddard, F G, *The Library Chronicle of The University of Texas* VIII, 4, Spring 1968

Unwin, Stanley; Mitchell, J; and Craigie, Sir William, *Iceland as we know it,* John Lane at Bodley Head, 1941

Whitehead, Kate, *The Third Programme: a Literary History,* Oxford University Press, 1989

Winchester, Simon, *Atlantic: a Vast Ocean of a Million Stories,* HarperPress, 2010

Wrigley, Amanda, and Harrison, S J (eds.), *Louis MacNeice: the Classical Radio Plays,* Oxford University Press, 2013

Note on other sources

Since my schooldays I have kept a commonplace book into which I have written excerpts from my reading that have struck a chord. I have used some of those, with whatever attribution and transcription errors made when I originally copied the excerpt down.

Thank you

In Austin: a big thank you to Liz and Eric at the Adams House B&B who provided the ideal base for my manuscript delving and a launchpad for my writing year; I enjoyed eating/watching the world go by at Snack Bar, Lamberts, Caffé Medici, Mother's Cafe, Dolce Vita, Hyde Park Bar & Grill, and Quack's 43rd St. Bakery; and I enjoyed soundtracks for the fortnight at the Continental Club, Waterloo Records and ACL Live. It is no reflection on them that I did not buy a belt in Allens Boots or a hat in Goorin Brothers or a book from BookPeople.

In Charlotte: best wishes for continued success to the Carolinas Latin Dance Company; I enjoyed eating at the Rock Bottom Brewery and Restaurant and Dandelion Market, pottering on the Fourth Ward garden tour and learning at the Levine Museum of the New South.

In Wilmington: I enjoyed eating at The Basics, The Wilmington Tea Room and Elijah's, browsing the two sisters bookery and learning at Cape Fear Museum and Wilmington Railroad Museum. Thanks to Best Western Coastline Inn, Bellamy Mansion Museum and Capt Maffitt's river cruise for their helpful flexibility.

On the north Atlantic: thank you to Andy and Richard at Strand Travel, thank you to Captain Roman and the officers and crew of *Julius S* (and my apologies if I misunderstood anything).

In London: thank you to my neighbours for keeping an eye on my house while I was away and to Stewart and Sara for giving an off-road parking space to my car while I travelled. Thank you to the Southbank Centre for the invitation to sit in on Marin Alsop's rehearsal with the Sao Paulo Symphony Orchestra and the Swingle Singers. In Oxford: thank you for a table in the Missing Bean. In Birmingham: apologies to Mary Moore (blue badge guide) for any details I may have misunderstood; and I enjoyed not drinking coffee at Yorks Bakery Cafe.

In Iceland: thanks to Magnus who helped make Snorri's Guesthouse in Reykjavik an excellent base for my time in Iceland and to Siggi, Svava and the yoga students for sharing their tour of Snaefellsnes with me. I enjoyed eating (in Reykjavik) at Sjavargrillid, at Glo and at Caruso, (in Akureyri) at Blaa Kannan and (in Isafjordur) at Edinborg and Braedraborg Café. I enjoyed concerts in Reykjavik's Hallgrimskirkja and Café Haiti and enjoyed learning (in Reykjavik) at the National Museum of Iceland, the Settlement Exhibition, the Culture House and the Kjarvalsstadir of Reykjavik's Art Museum and at the Westfjord Heritage Museum in Isafjordur. My personal favourite swimming pool (of the four I sampled) was at Sudureyri; pottering in Akureyri's Botanical Garden was relaxing and I finally found the Reykjavik coffee places I was looking for at Reykjavik Roasters and at Stofan Café.

In the Republic of Ireland: Foyle's Hotel in Clifden was a fitting base for my Connemara visit; I appreciated finding The Ennis Bookshop.

In New York state: The Milburn in New York City and the DoubleTree in Amherst were well-located for what I was doing and had just the facilities I wanted. Walking the Fall Creek Gorge trails on Cornell's campus gave me exercise, fresh air and new ideas. Thank you to the residents in the Fall 2013 semester of Telluride House at Cornell for their hospitality and conversations.

On the web: thanks to the twitter feed of @corrie_corfield that kept me posted (wherever in the world I was) on the weather and on the philosophers of the Northern Line and to the entertainment provided by the obliquely unofficial updates from @TlfTravelAlerts

My thanks to the many people who helped me with tourist and local information throughout my writing year, particularly those in Belfast and Carrickfergus, to the team at the London Library and to the community of librarians, curators and archivists at the Harry Ransom Humanities Research Center, University of Texas, Austin; the Rare Book & Manuscript Library in the Butler Library, Columbia University; the archives at Sarah Lawrence College; the Rockefeller Archive Center; the Carl A Kroch Library at Cornell University; and The Poetry Collection of the University Libraries and the University Archives of the State University of New York at Buffalo who, despite my non-academic background, gave me of their time and expertise to enrich my writing year.

In production: thank you to my beta readers Alethea Siow and particularly Linda Armitage and my mother, and thank you to Andy and Rich Carr for their guidance.

'And finally' (to use the phrase hallowed by the BBC): Thank you to all those individuals who have helped me in ways obvious and otherwise, so that you, reader, are now holding this book.

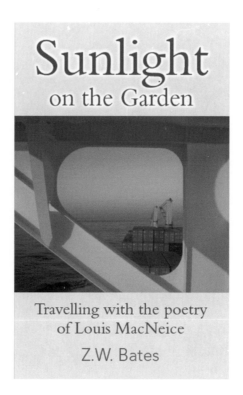